GOLDERS GREEN & HAMPSTEA[D]
VISIONS OF ARC[ADIA]

Adam Yamey is a London-based author and retired dental surgeon, who was brought up in Golders Green and Hampstead Garden Suburb. He is the author of several books including "Beneath a Wide Sky: Hampstead and its Environs", "Beyond Marylebone and Mayfair: Exploring West London". "Albania on my Mind", "Rediscovering Albania", "Charlie Chaplin waved to me", "Imprisoned in India", "Exodus to Africa", "Indian Freedom Fighters in London (1905-1910)", "Soap to Senate: A German Jew at the dawn of apartheid", "From Albania to Sicily", and "Scrabble with Slivovitz - Once upon a time in Yugoslavia". Adam lives in London. He is married and has one daughter.

Copyright © Adam Yamey, 2022

The moral right of the author has been asserted.

Unauthorised copying or modification of any of this part of this book

in any form or by any method

without the permission of the publisher is not permitted.

Published by Adam Yamey with Amazon KDP

ISBN 9798356367137

www.adamyamey.co.uk

GOLDERS GREEN & HAMPSTEAD GARDEN SUBURB: VISIONS OF ARCADIA

By

Adam Yamey

"Golders Green was a grassy cross-road

… All around us lay dairy farms, market gardens and

a few handsome old houses

… not far off there survived woods where we picked bluebells,

and streams by which we opened our picnic baskets."

Evelyn Waugh (1903-1966)

"Golders Green was, with the wind behind you,

only a ten-minute walk from Hampstead.

Our neighbours were always quick to point that out;

yet I have never heard anybody in Hampstead saying,

'We are quite close to Golders Green.'"

Dannie Abse (1923-2014)

Dedicated to the memory of my parents, Helen and Basil Yamey, who brought me up in our home in the Hampstead Garden Suburb.

TABLE OF CONTENTS

INTRODUCTION ... 7

THROUGH THE GARDEN SUBURB TO GOLDERS GREEN: MUTTON BROOK & THE RIVER BRENT ... 13

GOLDERS GREEN: ITS ORIGINS ... 39

JEWISH LIFE ... 49

RECOLLECTING GOLDERS GREEN ... 66

BRENT BRIDGE TO THE STATION ... 77

ONCE A COUNTRY TRACK: HOOP LANE ... 99

A GOLDERS GREEN VIGNETTE ... 107

FROM CHILDS HILL TO TEMPLE FORTUNE ... 109

UP NORTH END ROAD ... 127

HAMPSTEAD GARDEN SUBURB ('HGS') ... 141

    History ... 141

    Lutyens and Central Square ... 149

    Big and Little Woods ... 158

    HGS 'moderne', Market Place, and WW2 ... 161

    A stroll through the Suburb ... 171

    A HGS childhood ... 181

AFTERWORD ... 195

SOME BOOKS CONSULTED ... 199

ACKNOWLEDGEMENTS ... 201

INDEX ... 205

Golders Green war memorial clock tower and the station and train sheds behind it

INTRODUCTION

Golders Green is a bustling northwest London suburb. Its immediate neighbour, Hampstead Garden Suburb, is serene in comparison. The two areas began growing at the same time, as the result of a single important event. But their development followed very different paths. This book is about both places - past and present.

In 1907, trains began running on the newly opened extension of the Underground railway from Hampstead to Golders Green. They carried passengers between central London and Golders Green - a place which had been until then a rustic, almost arcadian part of the County of Middlesex. The establishment of a rapid commuter service to and from central London was the catalyst for the dramatic transformation of what had been a tiny rural hamlet into an extensive residential suburb. That same year, an area next to Golders Green began to be developed into a garden suburb. It was designed by a group of people with utopian ideals. This book explores both Golders Green and its distinctive neighbouring district, the Hampstead Garden Suburb.

The American columnist Bill Vaughan (1915-1977) wrote that a suburb:
"…is a place where someone cuts down all the trees to build houses, and then names the streets after the trees."

Fortunately, this was not the case with either Golders Green or Hampstead Garden Suburb: both are leafy to a greater or lesser extent. However, some of the streets in Golders Green are named after farms and large estates that were demolished when the place became transformed into a London suburb.

A poster issued in 1908 to attract families to dwell in the new suburb of Golders Green, to which the Underground railway had just been extended, bears the following lines from a poem, "The Task", written by William Cowper (1731-1800):

> "'Tis pleasant through the loopholes of retreat
> To peep at such a world; to see the stir
> Of the great Babel and not feel the crowd;
> To hear the roar she sends through all her gates
> At a safe distance, where the dying sound
> Falls a soft murmur on the uninjured ear."

These words were quoted because the poster's unknown artist wanted to compare the new suburban district to a sanctuary - a peaceful haven away from the hectic city.

Golders Green was such a retreat prior to 1907. It is near to the centre of London, yet feels so far away from it. Even now that it has become a bustling place, it still feels quite different to the heart of the city. Since its establishment in 1907, Hampstead Garden Suburb has never ceased to feel remote from the 'roar' of the city.

Golders Green lies beyond the hills north of Hampstead on the gently sloping south bank of the River Brent, a tributary of the River Thames. The Brent, which meets the Thames at Brentford, is formed at the edge of Golders Green where two of its tributaries, Dollis Brook and Mutton

Brook, meet. Mutton Brook and the Brent form parts of the northern boundaries of Golders Green and the neighbouring Garden Suburb.

Mutton Brook, Golders Green, and the Hampstead Garden Suburb figured greatly in my childhood (during the 1950s and 1960s) and I have many memories of them, some of which I have included in this volume. Writing this book was stimulated both by nostalgia and, more importantly, by a desire to make 'my' part of north London better-known to its residents and its many visitors.

At the outset, I will address a question: is Hampstead Garden Suburb a part of Golders Green? As far as the postal authorities are concerned, Golders Green, Temple Fortune, and a large part of the Suburb fall into the same postal district: NW11 (the 'Golders Green district'). In terms of architecture, town planning and appearance, and less easily definable social aspects and attitudes, the part of NW11, which is commonly regarded as 'Golders Green' is quite distinct from the Hampstead Garden Suburb ('HGS').

My parents and an aunt, who lived in HGS, gave me the strong impression that they regarded Golders Green as being quite different from the Suburb. It used to annoy my aunt when, mischievously but correctly, I used to add 'Golders Green' as an address line when I sent her letters and postcards. But she was not alone in that respect.

The writer Evelyn Waugh (1903-1966) spent the early years of his life in a house his father had had built on North End Road between Golders Green and Hampstead before the Underground reached Golders Green.

He wrote in his autobiographical "A Little Learning" (published 1964) that following the arrival of the Underground, his father was dismayed to learn that his house fell into the newly created postal district of Golders Green, which to him meant the name of a 'tube' station. He would have preferred it to have been living in the postal district which contains Hampstead, a place which he associated with artistic giants such as Blake, Constable, and Keats. As for HGS, Evelyn quoted the following words by his father, who had had some differences of opinion with Henrietta Barnett, its founder:

"Blast it! Darn it!

Henrietta Elizabeth Barnett"

Despite this, his father eventually came to terms with having the HGS on his doorstep because:

"…he was drawn into the community later by church-going and his perennial delight in amateur theatricals."

Recently, the Borough of Barnet revised its wards' boundaries. 'Golders Green' became a separate ward from one named 'Garden Suburb', and others named 'Childs Hill' and 'East Finchley'. According to that definition, although next to Golders Green, HGS is in another ward. An answer to the question I posed is that Golders Green and HGS are completely distinct places, but within the same postal district.

Our exploration of what was once an Arcadian place near London commences with a chapter about two features of the landscape that existed long before human activity reached the present postal district of Golders Green: Mutton Brook and the River Brent.

The Kingsley Way bridge over Mutton Brook

THROUGH THE GARDEN SUBURB TO GOLDERS GREEN: MUTTON BROOK & THE RIVER BRENT

"Golders Green, a hamlet of Hendon, Middx, a little outlying cluster of cottages with an inn … lies along the main road, midway between Hampstead and Hendon, the little Brent brook forming its N. boundary…"

So wrote James Thorne in 1876. The brook to which he referred was the upper reaches of the River Brent, close to the point where its tributaries, Dollis Brook and Mutton Brook, meet. The latter flows through Hampstead Garden Suburb ('HGS'), where I was brought up.

Mutton Brook is a geographical feature that was in existence long before there was any human habitation in the Golders Green area. The stream's course might have originated because of the spread of an ice sheet (the Anglian Glaciation) as long ago as 450,000 years. Few, if any, people lived along the Brook until many centuries after the Roman Conquest. Scarcely any archaeological finds have been found near the Brook, and there is no evidence of early settlements beside it. This is in contrast with the mouth of the River Brent (at Brentford), where much evidence of human activity has been discovered, dating from even before the Roman conquest.

The origin of the stream's name remains obscure. Jackie Davey, writing about the still existing College Farm (on Finchley's Regents Park Road) that lies on a slope north of the Brook, noted (www.nlu3a.org.uk) that it was:

"… first called Sheep House Farm and was started by Adam de Basing, Lord of the Manor and a well beloved friend of Henry III … Adam de Basing was given permission to clear up to 250 acres of forest a year so that his sheep could roam freely. He was the only person allowed to keep sheep. Mutton Brook was used for dipping sheep…"

Adam de Basing, who died in about 1266, was Mayor of London in 1251. Basing Hill Park (established in the 1930s from what had formerly been agricultural fields) in Golders Green is probably named after him.

I will now describe a walk along Mutton Brook and the places through which it passes between its source and Golders Green. Most of the Brook can be seen from publicly accessible roads, footpaths, and open spaces. Only a few short stretches cannot be seen because they run underground or through private land.

Mutton Brook rises in Cherry Tree Wood (a remnant of the historic, mediaeval 'Finchley wood' that was once well-known for its highwaymen). According to a website (barnet.gov.uk), the wood:

"… had long been known as Dirt house Wood because the night soil and horse manure cleaned from London's streets was brought as fertiliser for the hay meadows to the Dirt house, now the White Lion public house next to the station."

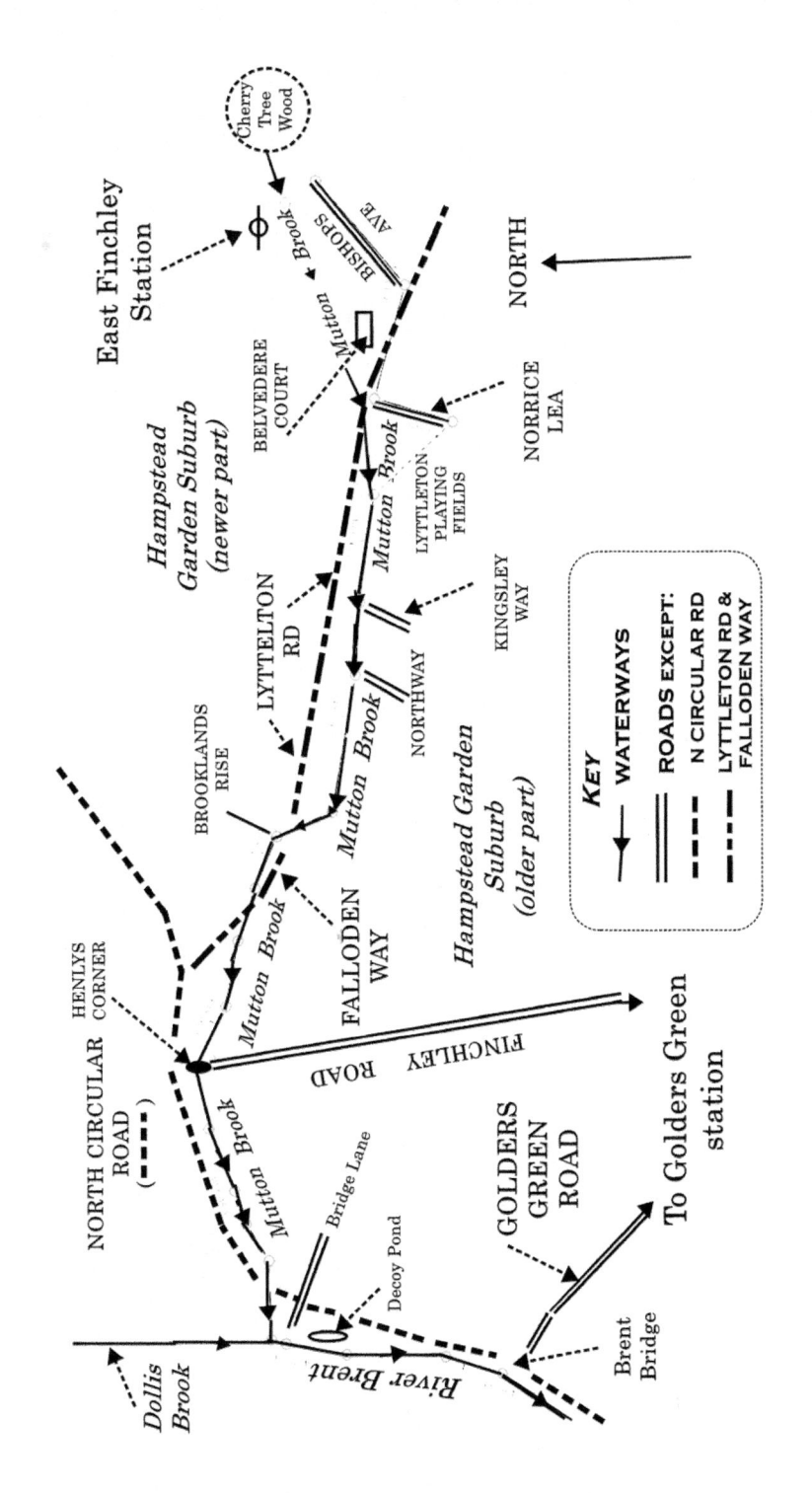

Schematic map of Mutton Brook: from its source to where the River Brent begins at Golders Green

Between the wood and Lyttelton Playing Fields (see below), the Brook is not accessible to the public. It runs west and slightly south from the wood, which is next to East Finchley Station where this perambulation begins.

East Finchley Underground station is above ground. Art Deco in design (architects: Charles Holden and LH Bucknell), it was built in the latter half of the 1930s. Holden (1875-1960) was involved in the design of many of London's Underground stations during the 1920s and 1930s. A ten-foot-tall sculpture of a kneeling archer, sculpted by Eric Aumonier (1899–1974) overlooks both the platforms and the station's forecourt. The significance of the archer is that East Finchley used to be at the edge of the ancient Royal Forest of Enfield where both royalty and commoners once hunted. Lovers of Art Deco should visit the Phoenix Cinema just north of the station. Opened in 1910, it has been screening films ever since then. It contains some Art Deco decorative features.

Bordering the station's car park and facing the A1000 (High Road, East Finchley), stands the head office of the UK section of the McDonalds 'fast-food' company. Next to the station, The Old White Lion pub, established by 1716, stands alongside The Great North Road (A1000). Formerly called 'The Dirt House' for the reason already given, it was a coaching inn where the teams of horses pulling the Manchester Mail were first changed after leaving London. Until 1900, there was a tollgate on the Great North Road next to the pub. The hostelry's current (20th century) building has some interesting eye-shaped features in its roof tiling. These roof slits resemble those found on many old buildings in Central and Eastern Europe.

East Finchley Underground station

Eye-like slits in the roof of The Old White Lion pub in East Finchley

The western part of Bishops Avenue is home to wealthy people who live in large, mostly tastelessly adorned, opulent houses. It leads from the A1000 to Aylmer Road (part of the A1). The avenue, which was always intended to be for expensive houses, was laid out in about 1887 on land which had once been part of the Bishop of London's hunting park (the bishop was also the Lord of the Manor of Finchley). It cut through the Bishop's Wood and farmland north of it, and runs all the way to the edge of the grounds of Kenwood House.

Belvedere Court on Aylmer Road is an unmissable long, brick and stone building with an un-British appearance. This block of flats, built 1937-38 in the Art Deco ('moderne') style, was designed by the psychoanalyst Sigmund Freud's youngest son, the architect Ernst Ludwig Freud (1892-1970). Born in Vienna, he attended the Vienna Polytechnic and then was privately trained by the architect Adolf Loos (1870-1933), a pioneer of modern architecture. Ernst was also influenced by Mies Van der Rohe (1886-1969). Well-established as an architect in Germany, Ernst came to the UK with his father in 1934. Belvedere Court was advanced for its time as this excerpt from the historicengland.org.uk website revealed:

"The plan comprises three linked blocks in slightly canted formation; entrances at ends and in centre of blocks, with seven staircases each giving access to two flats on each of the four floors. At rear are garages and stores, with trades' hoists served by their own intercom and dust chutes, off recessed kitchen balconies … The whole concept was of 'truly labour saving flats' in fashionable surroundings, offering a continental lifestyle ideally suited to the many refugees then escaping central Europe for north London. The flats were originally designed for rent, not for sale."

At first, the flats in this building were rented mainly to Jewish immigrants fleeing from Nazi-occupied Europe. During his childhood, the TV personality Jerry Springer (born 1944 in Highgate Underground station, where his mother was sheltering during an air-raid) lived in Belvedere Court.

West of Belvedere Court, a road called Norrice Lea runs south through Hampstead Garden Suburb ('HGS') from Aylmer Road. The word 'lea' means 'a clearing' or 'open ground' in Old English. HGS United Synagogue is on Norrice Lea. Its 'modern Orthodox' congregation was founded in 1934. The synagogue was designed by Maurice de Metz and completed in 1935. With its elegant, neo-classical main portico, it was consecrated in 1934, and then, after sustaining war damage, it was enlarged far less elegantly in the 1960s. An unusual feature of this synagogue is that The Ark (housing the Torah scrolls) faces west instead of the conventional east. The reason for this (according to hgsheritage.org.uk) is as follows:

"The site at Norrice Lea faced East and therefore if the Ark was placed in the East (facing Jerusalem as is the custom) it would occupy the front position of the site. It was not, however, practicable to have the entrance of the Synagogue at the rear of this site, and accordingly the Ark faced West, as indeed it still does in the Synagogue today."

A short (75 yards) inaccessible stretch of Mutton Brook runs north of the synagogue between Norrice Lea and Lyttelton Playing Fields. A narrow pathway, about 150 yards south of the synagogue, leads from Norrice Lea between private gardens and into Lyttelton Playing Fields. From there, we can enjoy an excellent view across this grassy expanse. The higher parts of HGS and its churches (St Judes with its spire and The Free Church with its dome; and between them with a short tower, The Institute) can be seen.

Enter the Playing Fields and head for the small café, which shares premises with a Jewish kindergarten. The school is protected by security guards when the children are attending classes. A short path leads a few feet northwards from the café to a small, hump-backed bridge. It is from this brick-walled bridge that we can first catch sight of Mutton Brook. Confined between banks maintained with wooden planking and lined with bushes on both sides, the Brook is no more than about two feet wide at this point. By the time that the Brook reaches the next bridge, the brick and stone structure, which carries Kingsley Way over the water, its width has almost doubled. A gauge next to the latter bridge projects vertically from the water. Its presence suggests that the brook can become much deeper during times of heavy rainfall.

View of Hampstead Garden Suburb from
Lyttelton Playing Fields: St Judes on the left; Free Church on the right.

Hampstead Garden Suburb Synagogue on Norrice Lea

Near the bridge and within HGS, there are a few houses with Art Deco features, notably their upper storey windows. These buildings, constructed in 1934, are on Kingsley Close. They have curved suntrap windows with metal frames made by Crittall (a company which has been making steel framed windows since the 1880s). These homes were designed by the architects Herbert Welch (1884–1953), Nugent Francis Cachemaille-Day (1896–1976), and Felix Lander (1890-1960). Welch designed many buildings in HGS and in nearby Golders Green. Near the meeting of Kingsley Way and the Market Place (Lyttelton Road), there used to be a delicatessen, Cohens, where my parents bought smoked salmon occasionally in the early 1960s. In those days, this delicacy was far more of a luxury than it is now.

Market Place is lined with shops and cafés, which have flats above them. The road (Lyttleton Road and its continuation Falloden Way) along which they stand separates Hampstead Garden Suburb into two distinct areas. It is the only part of the Suburb containing shops. The section of HGS to the north of Market Place was built later than most of the Suburb south of it. In the 1950s, there had been plans to make Lyttelton Road part of a 'Lorry Route' serving London's docks. However, by 1968 the plans for what would have been a noisome addition to the neighbourhood, had been abandoned.

Mutton Brook flows over many small waterfalls along its short (just over 2 miles) course. After passing over a small waterfall, the stream flows under the Kingsley Way bridge, and then exits it after tumbling down two more step-like waterfalls. Then it flows towards Northway in a stone-lined channel that curves sinuously through a strip of cultivated parkland. When I was a child, there was a small public putting-green in this park, but that has gone. The single-arched bridge carrying Northway over the stream has iron railings. The water flows next through Northway Gardens between almost vertical banks, like a groove neatly cut into the lawns. It passes some tennis courts on its left bank, and tumbles over another low waterfall. The Gardens, which vary in width, are flanked to the north by the back gardens of houses on Falloden Way (the westerly continuation of Lyttelton Road). To the south, they meet the bottom ends of the gardens of houses on Oakwood Road.

The Brook curves northwards and then disappears under Falloden Way, beneath a bridge with brick walls topped with white stone slabs. Before doing so, it passes a notice that warns passers-by of the risk of flooding. It emerges from under the main road divided into two channels that soon merge into one. Brooklands Drive crosses the Brook over a bridge made from wood and bricks. The stream then flows over another waterfall before entering a concrete-lined conduit that carries it back under Falloden Way. Between its emergence from under Falloden Way and where Finchley Road crosses it, Mutton Brook winds its way between steeply sloping meadows on its right bank and wooded land on its left bank. Walking beside it, one could imagine that one is in the middle of the countryside, if it were not for the sight of, and muted sounds of traffic moving along Falloden Way. Long ago, it is likely that sheep grazed on this bank of the Brook.

At Finchley Road, the Brook flows unceremoniously beneath the roadway near to what used to be known in my childhood as 'Henlys Corner'. Many years earlier (in 1908), when the Catholic Father Bendon arrived in the area, there were watercress beds at what became Henlys Corner. No doubt, these water-loving plants were irrigated with water from Mutton Brook. The busy traffic intersection was named after Henlys Garage that used to stand there between 1935 and 1989. Henlys was a major motor car distributor and dealer, founded in 1917 and then taken over by another company in the 1980s.

The Kinloss Schul (synagogue)

La Delivrance ('The Naked Lady')

Finchley Road continues across the North Circular Road and becomes 'Regents Park Road'. A spectacular sculpture, depicting a naked lady holding a sword aloft, stands on a traffic island immediately north of the Henlys Corner junction. This is the 'La Délivrance' statue (aka 'The Naked Lady'), sculpted by the French artist Emile Guillaume (1867-1942), a pacifist. It is a cast made from the original that was exhibited in the Paris Salon in 1920, where it was seen by the proprietor of the Daily Mail newspaper, Viscount Rothermere (1868-1940). He commissioned the manufacture of the cast of the lady, who stands looking north towards Finchley with her backside pointing towards Temple Fortune and the North Circular Road. She was unveiled in 1927 by a former prime minister, David Lloyd-George (1863-1945). Close to the Naked Lady stands the 'Kinloss Schul' also known as 'Finchley United Synagogue'. It is a striking building with its multiple external vertical reinforced concrete elements. Home to one of Europe's largest Jewish congregations and capable of accommodating two thousand people, this edifice was completed in 1967 by the architects Dowton and Hurst.

Mutton Brook continues west of Finchley Road almost parallel to the North Circular Road. This highway was constructed in the 1920s and 1930s both as a bypass of Central London and to connect local industrial areas. In the 1950s, it was extended to reach the river Thames east of the city. Now, this busy route runs from Chiswick in the west to Silvertown in the east. In complete contrast, Mutton Brook flows through pleasantly rustic-looking parkland, lawns, and woods, until it reaches a point where the North Circular Road begins curving in a south-westerly direction. After passing a fading sign that declares "Polluted Water Keep Out", both the footpath and the brook pass under the main road in a large diameter concrete-lined tunnel, circular in cross-section. This is surveyed by a cobwebbed CCTV camera. The footpath follows the Brook for about one third of a mile from the tunnel before reaching the last bridge that crosses it. This footbridge with wrought-iron railings crosses the stream a few feet from the point where it joins Dollis Brook at right angles. The waters from the two streams mingle to become the River Brent.

A few yards away from the meeting of its tributaries, the River Brent flows under a road bridge with white stone balustrades. This bridge marks the end of Bridge Lane, which begins in Temple Fortune. After crossing the bridge, the road becomes Bell Lane, which leads north towards central Hendon. Bridge Lane is marked on a detailed map drawn in 1864. It is shown crossing the Brent on a bridge then named 'Mutton Bridge'. Temple Fortune, now a flourishing shopping area, is so named because it is on land once owned by the Knights Templar. The word 'fortune' probably derives from 'foran tun', which meant 'a settlement in front of, or before, the main one' (the 'main one' being either Hendon or Finchley). A website (barnet.gov.uk) noted:

"By the end of the 18th century, Temple Fortune Farm was established on the northern side of Farm Close … Temple Fortune Farm was removed to build the Arcade and Gateway House (c1911). Although the area had horse drawn omnibuses as early as the 1880s, it was the tramline of 1910 from Church End Finchley to Golders Green Station that led to house building in the area west of the Finchley Road. The Carmelite Monastery was established in Bridge Lane in 1908. Golders Green Police Station was opened in Temple Fortune in 1913."

The police station, which existed during my childhood is no longer present in Temple Fortune in its former location south of Bridge Lane. The elegant brick building that housed it (1096 Finchley Road) still exists. As for the Carmelite Monastery, its former home (on Havannah Drive, which leads off Bridge Lane, close to the North Circular) has been converted into a complex of houses and flats, a gated community, called Carmel Gate. Some of its original external architectural features have been preserved. Before Finchley Road was built in about 1827, a country track, Ducksetters Lane, ran between Temple Fortune and Finchley.

At Bridge Lane (probably named because of the bridge crossing the Brent), the 'young' river is many times broader than Mutton Brook was at Lyttelton Playing Fields about 2 miles upstream. After crossing Bridge Lane, a footpath enters Brent River Park, which, like all the green areas that have been described already, is maintained by the London Borough of Barnet. The River Brent flows along the northern edge of this strip of parkland, which runs almost parallel to the North Circular Road until it meets the A40. A more picturesque name for this busy road might be 'The Brent Valley Highway'.

The Decoy Pond

Brent River Park, which forms part of the northern boundary of Golders Green, was opened to the public in 1934. It is on land that was part of both the grounds of Brent Bridge House (demolished 1935) and part of Decoy Farm (no longer in existence). The park contains a piece of water of historic interest: the Decoy Pond. Decoy ponds were used to capture waterfowl for food. When the birds entered such a pond, the hunters lured them with food to narrow inlets where they were easily trapped in tapering nets. The age of the pond is uncertain, but by 1754 there was a house 'Decoy House', named after the pond, in existence. The pond is now a good place to spot a variety of waterfowl including ducks, moorhens, coots, and herons. It is surrounded by decorative iron benches in various states of disrepair. Each of them bears the coat of arms of the Borough of Barnet. While the waters of the pond are placid, and often covered in many places with a good growth of green weeds, the Brent that flows past its northern edge is quite a torrent in comparison. At one point, the river drops about five feet over a spectacular waterfall. Meanwhile, on the south side of the pond, but high above it, traffic rushes along the North Circular. Oddly, this hardly disturbs the peace of the lovely park.

Mutton Brook passing through the tunnel beneath the North Circular Road

Pedestrian bridge across the North Circular Road at the north end of Golders Green Road

Ruined gazebo in the grounds of the former Brent Bridge House

The south end of Brent Street, which begins in Hendon, meets the north end of Golders Green Road on a brick bridge with wrought-iron railings, which traverses the Brent. It is marked on old maps as 'Brent Bridge'. Beyond this, the river flows south-westwards between the back gardens of buildings on both sides of it, and there is no footpath to follow. On the eastern side of the bridge, and only just visible through the dense vegetation, the river flows through a narrow artificial weir built between two ruined circular towers covered with graffiti. Each of these, which I last saw in 2017, has a conical roof with several tiles missing. They appear to have been designed as viewing points or gazebos. They stand in what used to be the grounds of Brent Bridge House, which was an 18th century stuccoed building, once the seat of the Whishaws. Charles Whishaw had converted it from a farmhouse into a 'gentleman's residence' by 1828. A barrister and anti-slavery activist John Whishaw (c1764-1840) lived there. Later, parts of this building were incorporated into the Brent Bridge Hotel (opened just before 1914). In 1963, eleven years before it was demolished, my parents spent a few nights in the hotel whilst our damp house in Hampstead Garden Suburb was being dried out. It had been left unheated during the three winter months that we had spent in the USA.

Moving southeast from Brent Bridge, we reach Golders Green. Before exploring it and its people, let us first look at the history of this place that rapidly became one of northwest London's important transport hubs and a busy commercial centre.

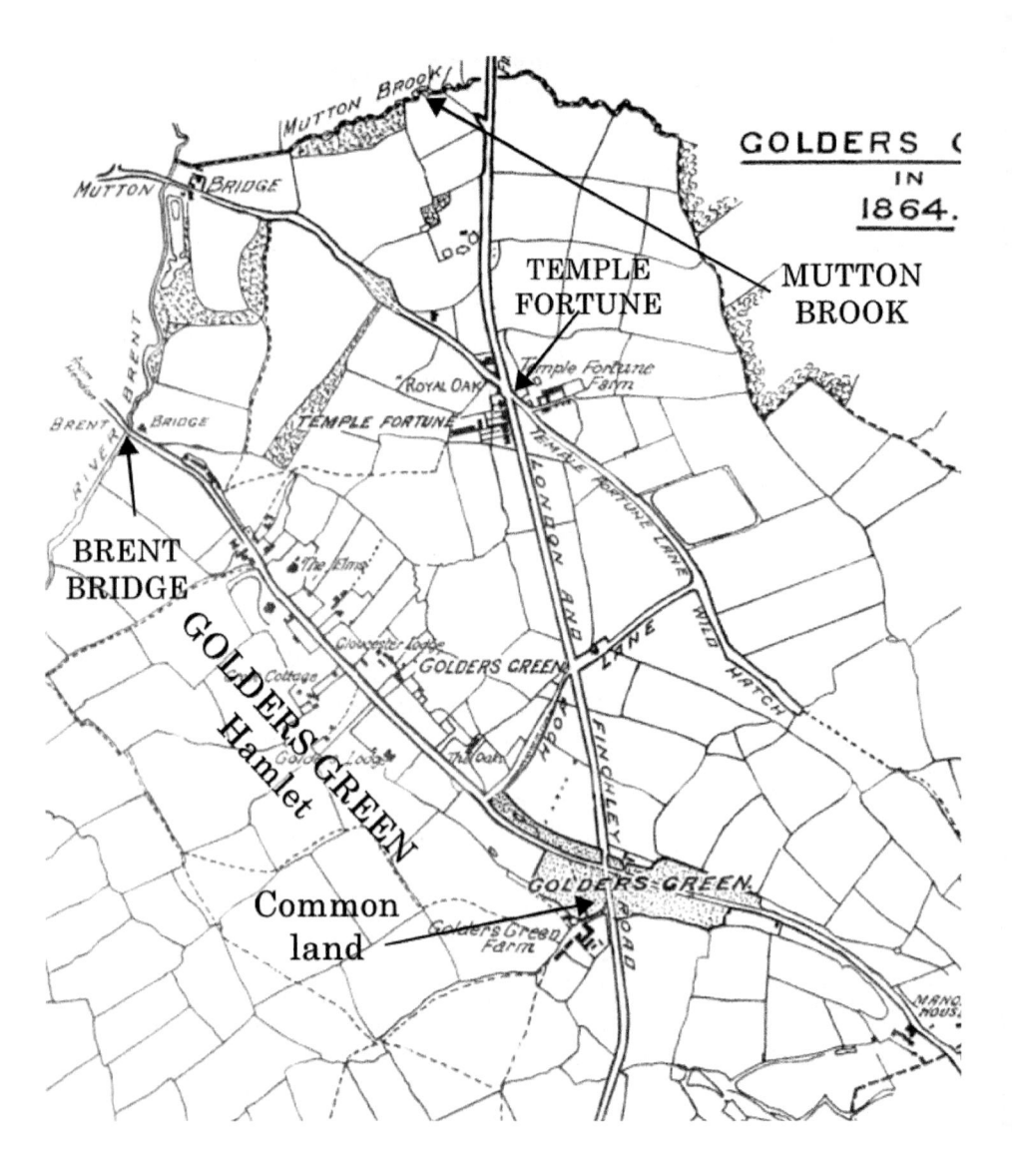

Golders Green in 1864
(Map adapted from Howitt's 1923 book)

GOLDERS GREEN: ITS ORIGINS

Before delving into its distant past, here is what Edward Walford (1823-1897) wrote about Golders Green as it was in in about 1883 when he published his book "Village London. Part 1":

"… a bridge over the river Brent leads to Golders Green, another hamlet of Hendon, which is pleasantly located on the road to Hampstead.

Golders Green consists of a few decent cottages and villa residences fringing the roadside, the larger part of the 'green' proper being now enclosed. The 'White Swan' tavern, with its tea gardens is a favourite resort of London holiday-makers in the summer-time, the various walks by rural lanes and field-paths in the immediate neighbourhood adding much to the charm of the locality."

And this is how the author Evelyn Waugh (1903-1966) remembered it was when he was about four years old. Writing in 1964, he recalled:

"Golders Green was a grassy cross-road … All around us lay dairy farms, market gardens and a few handsome old houses of brick or stucco standing in twenty acres or more; not far off there survived woods where we picked bluebells, and streams by which we opened our picnic baskets."

Francis Howkins, author of the detailed "The Story of Golders Green" (published 1923), pointed out that the early history of Golders Green is that of the Manor of Hendon, of which it was a part. Although Hendon was mentioned in the 11th century Domesday Book, Golders Green was not. In about 1150, Abbot Gervais de Blois (c1115-1160), an illegitimate son of King Stephen, granted a large part of his Hendon property to Gilbert Fitz Gunter. About 100 years later, this land was held by a man called Le Rous, and his family married into the De Brent family, who had a home close to the River Brent. The land (i.e., the manor) passed through many hands until it was purchased in about 1756 by the actor David Garrick (1717-1779), who also bought Hendon Hall (in Parson Street, Hendon) as an investment (he never lived there). Howkins suggested that Garrick would have been seen riding along what is now called Golders Green Road while travelling between his hall and Central London. Gradually, the manor (to quote Howkins):

"… gradually decreased as property passed, either by agreement or otherwise, to other owners until only a few freehold fields remained to the Lord … But even today there are many people in Golders Green who own their freehold houses, and yet the 'minerals in the ground' still remain vested in the Lords of the Manor."

I am not sure who owns these 'minerals in the ground' today.

The name 'Goulders Green' was noted by William Camden (1551-1623) in the late 16th century. Goulder might have been a local landowner. When the French cartographer John Rocque (c1704-1762) drew his detailed maps of London in 1741-1745, he marked what is now Golders Green as 'Groles Green'. The Survey of English Place Names (http://epns.nottingham.ac.uk) noted that Golders Green was recorded as

'Golders Greene' in 1612 and 1619; as 'Goulders Green in 1680; as 'Groles Green' in 1754; as 'Groles' or 'Godders' Green in 1790; and as 'Goldhurst Green' in 1790. The Survey remarked:

"The first element is clearly a personal name. No surname Golder has been noted in any record relating to the parish, but ... we have mention of John le Godere (1321) and in 1371 ... of John Godyer of Hendon. Nearby is Golders Hill in Finchley ... which is Godereshill ... It may well be that the green and hill alike took their name from this family God (y)ere, with later corruption to Golder in both cases."

The pre-20th century growth of the hamlet has been reported as follows (www.british-history.ac.uk/vch/middx/vol5/):

"By 1754 there were about 16 houses with small gardens at Golders Green, near the later site of the Underground station, most of them on small inclosures from the waste. In 1814 Golders Green contained 'many ornamental villas and cottages, surrounded with plantations', and in 1828 detached houses spread on both sides of the road as far as Brent bridge. The green, already much attenuated, was finally inclosed in 1873-4."

The 'green' itself was the area around where the station is currently located, and where Finchley Road intersects the old North End Road (now North End Road and its western continuation, Golders Green Road) between Hampstead and Hendon. Until the arrival of the Underground in 1907 (see below), most of the small settlement of Golders Green was strung along what is now Golders Green Road between Hoop Lane and Brent Bridge. Where Golders Green Road meets Finchley Road (close to the clock tower), there was the green, and a nearby farm (marked as 'Golders Green Farm' on a map surveyed in 1864, and as 'Hodford Farm' on a map drawn 30 years later; there is now a Hodford Road in this area). The settlement, as marked on the detailed 1864 map, consisted of a smithy amongst a small collection of buildings known as 'Albert Row' near the Brent; another short terrace of houses; and several large houses set in their own extensive grounds (e.g., Alba Lodge, The Elms, Grove House, Stilton Lodge, Gloucester Lodge, Golders Lodge, and The Oaks). Thirty years later, a map surveyed in 1891-94 showed that a few more of these substantial houses and 'lodges' had been built.

An advertisement in the London "Times" of the 13th of April 1872 regarding the sale of Golders Lodge illustrated the substantial nature of this kind of dwelling:

"… comprising 13 bedrooms and dressing rooms, bathroom, entrance hall, dining and drawing rooms, two breakfast rooms, study, dressing room, and lavatory, and the most complete domestic offices, with coach house, stabling etc. The grounds are tastefully disposed, in lawns, flower gardens, kitchen garden, conservatory, potting-shed, plantation, and paddock, all in about three acres, the whole possessing frontage to the high road of about 520 feet…"

Another property sales notice ("Times", 16th of April 1885) revealed that The Elms had amongst its amenities 16 bedrooms, a cowhouse, a coach house for five carriages, as well as rooms for grooms.

The existence of lavish residences such as this required the employment of many servants. The "Times" was full of advertisements seeking such employees (for work in Golders Green) during the last three decades of the 19th century. By then, a short terrace of small houses, still in existence (see below), had been built quite a distance from the rest of Golders Green, east of Finchley Road on what is now North End Road.

To summarise: until the end of the 19th century, Golders Green was no more than a sparsely populated rural hamlet on the country road running from Hampstead to Hendon. This situation continued unchanged until 1907.

Golders Green's centuries' long existence as a rustic hamlet ended abruptly when the extension of the Northern Line of the Underground (from Hampstead) reached it, and began carrying passengers in 1907. What is now the Northern Line, but was then the 'Charing Cross, Euston & Hampstead Railway', rises from about 20 feet below sea level at Embankment station to about 220 feet above sea level at Golders Green. The platforms at Hampstead are 192 feet below ground level, the ground in that part of Hampstead being almost 400 feet above sea level. Golders Green station is at ground level and open-air. To reach it from Hampstead, the line ascends gradually, passing below a ridge of hills, The Northern Heights, which reaches an altitude of 440 feet (near Whitestone Pond). It was this ridge running between Hampstead and Highgate, which inhibited the spread of London beyond Hampstead towards Golders Green (and Hendon) before the 'tube' line was constructed. Work on the two tunnels between Hampstead and Golders green commenced in 1903. They were bored by 1905, but not ready for trains until two years later. The station was inaugurated on the 22nd of June 1907. It was opened officially by David Lloyd-George (1863-1945), then the President of the Board of Trade, and later (1916-1922) Prime Minister.

The extension of the tube line to Golders Green was inspired by an American financier, Charles Tyson Yerkes (1837-1905), who had already developed mass transit systems in Philadelphia and Chicago. He had realised that by creating these methods of travel and extending them into the countryside, potentially lucrative suburban development would soon follow. An article published on the www.businessinsider.com website in December 2014 recorded:

"On August 3rd, 1900, Charles Yerkes, an American financier and ex-convict, gazed across London from the top of Hampstead Heath. His journey through the capital in a horse-drawn carriage had already begun to persuade him that it was a fine place to invest. The streets heaved with people; Yerkes had never travelled through such a densely populated city. But the view from one of its highest points clinched his interest.

To the south lay spires, crowded terraced houses and congested streets. To the north were pastures, stretches of farmland and a few sleepy villages. Within two decades that landscape was transformed - thanks to Yerkes. By 1907 elegant redbrick Underground stations had been built to the north at Archway, near Highgate village, and to the north-west at Golders Green … Land values surged. A photograph of Golders Green from 1920 shows an elegant high street lined with four-storey buildings and bustling with cars and buses."

According to a history of the Northern Line (https://content.tfl.gov.uk/research-guide-no-13-a-brief-history-of-the-northern-line.pdf):

"The Charing Cross, Euston and Hampstead railway had its origins in a Bill as far back as 1892. However, until the arrival of the American financier Charles Tyson Yerkes in 1899, the scheme was stalled for want of money to fund the construction contracts. With his contacts and knowledge of the mechanics of raising these sums, the line was built and opened in June 1907 between Charing Cross in the south, Golders Green and Highgate (now Archway) in the north, with a junction at Camden Town."

Various Acts of Parliament were passed, notably those in 1902 and 1903, which paved the way for the extension of the railway to Golders Green and beyond.

Howitt related:

"From the year 1905 the green fields of Golders Green were destined to be covered with bricks and mortar."

Unlike Yerkes, some property developers looked on the prospect of a new suburb at Golders Green with scepticism. Others, as Howitt noted:

"… seem to have been led by a kind of blind faith that here, if anywhere, would boldness, energy, and work be remunerated, and these had a saying that there was Gold in Golders Green".

And they were not mistaken. Improvements in the area's infrastructure were required to allow for what was soon to be a massive increase in Golders Green's population and housing density. Finchley Road was improved to accommodate trams (in 1910) and the 'omnibus' services that linked Golders Green with Finchley (to the north) and the West End via Swiss Cottage (to the south). As noted by Howitt, at the beginning of the 20th century:

"… Golders Green was awakening from a long sleep, and was about to take a very active part in helping the growth of Greater London."

Curiously, the first new house to be built in Golders Green (in 1905) was not close to the new station, but north of it where Hoop Lane crosses Finchley Road. This dull looking but historic edifice is now part of a hotel (currently, the Oyo Central).

A series of maps drawn in 1907, 1912, and 1923 (when Howitt's book was published) illustrate Golders Green's extremely rapid growth, as well as that of Temple Fortune and Childs Hill (south of Golders Green). These three former hamlets had become merged into a single urban conglomeration by the 1920s. However, west of this urban settlement, there was still open countryside in 1923: these fields have largely been covered with buildings and roads since then.

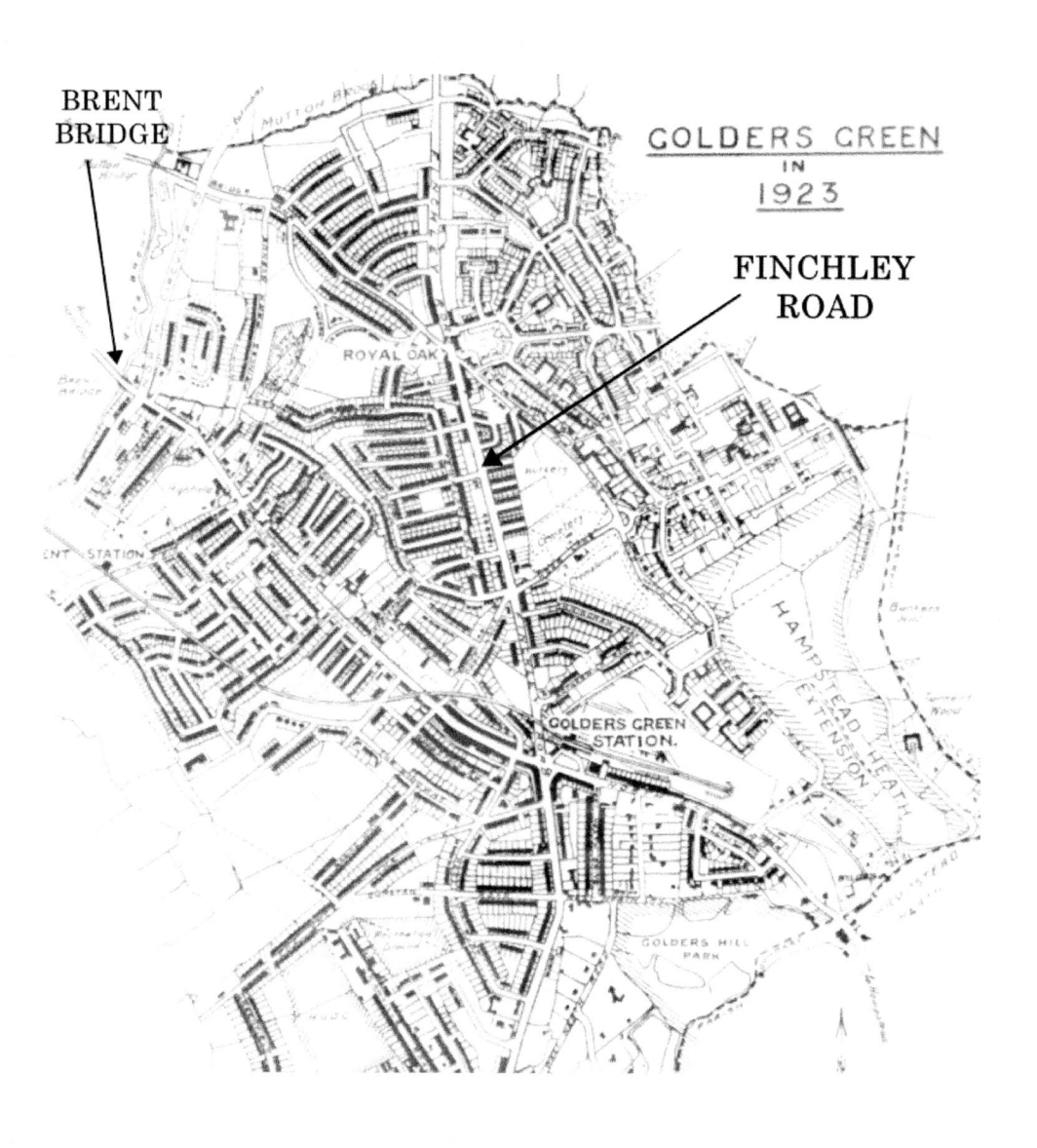

Map of Golders Green in 1923
(adapted from Howitt)

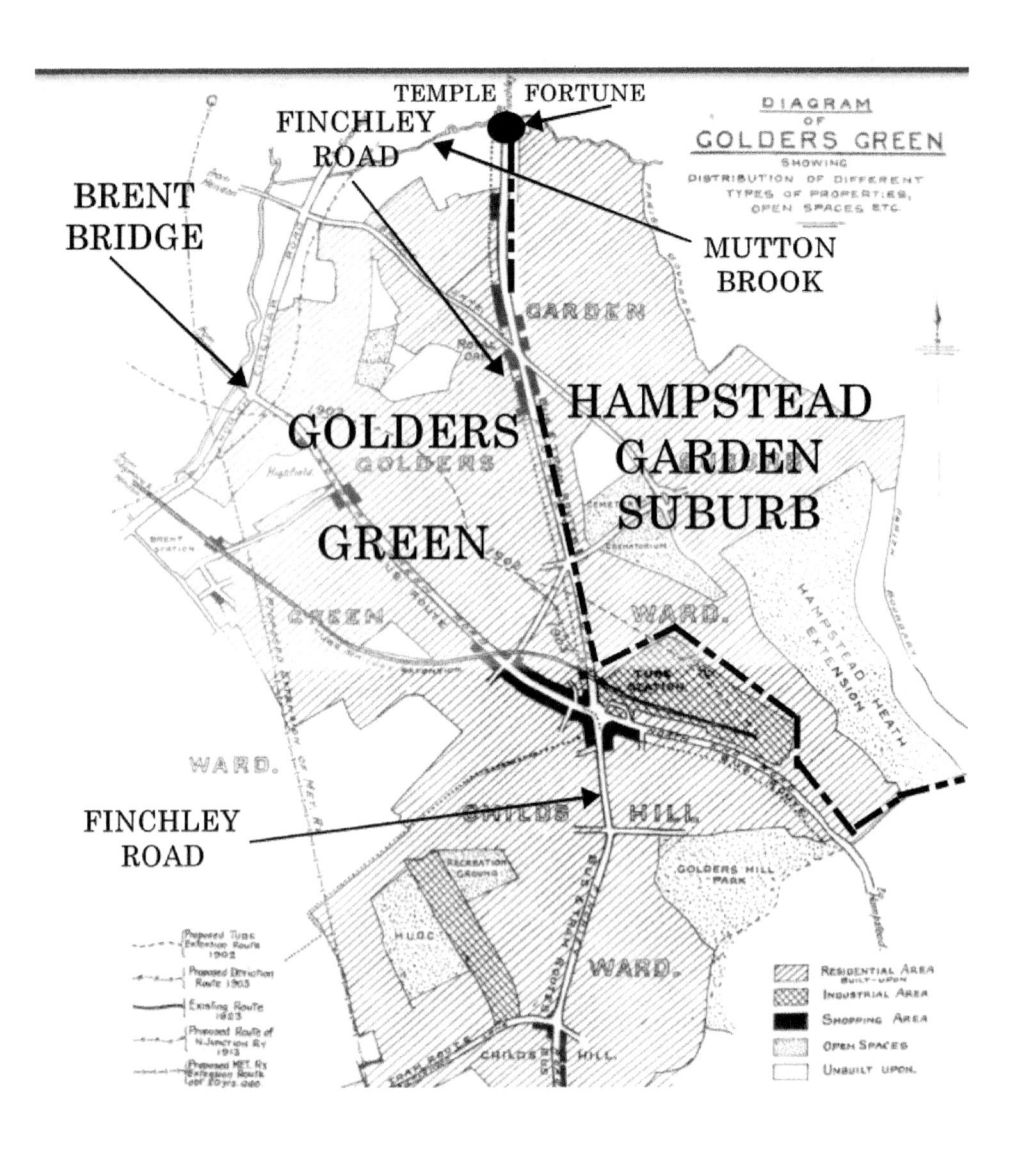

Golders Green and Hampstead Garden Suburb in 1923
(Adapted from Howitt)

JEWISH LIFE

Golders Green is associated with the presence of a substantial population of Jewish people. I cannot find any reference to this in Howitt's book (published in 1923). As Pam Fox has written an informative book called "The Jewish Community of Golders Green: A Social History" (published in 2016), I shall only discuss selected aspects of the Jewish presence in the area.

Ms Fox noted that before 1907, there were only a few Jewish people living in Golders Green. One of them was a famous art dealer. His nephew James Henry Duveen, writing in his "The Rise of the House of Duveen" (published in 1957), recalled:

"At the suggestion of my uncle Joel, I was sent to England to sell old Dutch furniture to the dealers. I was then in my seventeenth year. Before starting on my business journey I stayed two days with my uncle at his country house, 'The Hawthorns,' opposite what is now Golders Green Station, London."

Joel's uncle with a country retreat in Golders Green was the Dutch born Jewish art dealer Sir Joseph Joel Duveen (1843-1908), who financed the building of a lavish extension to the Tate Gallery (now 'Tate Britain'). He moved from his native Holland to London in 1878. Knighted in the year that he died, Sir Joseph was, according to Fox, the first Jewish person to live in Golders Green. I do not know when Duveen moved into The Hawthorns, but a notice published in the "Times" on the 5th of September 1885 revealed:

"… Early English House, of red brick, built 1882. Contains, on ground floor, three reception rooms, lavatory, two water closets, kitchen … first floor six bedrooms … two good attics, and large bedroom … good cellar, wine cellar, coal cellar … Tennis lawn, shrubberies, and garden planted with fruit trees … Apply to S.G., The Hawthorns, Golders-Green, Finchley Road, London NW…"

I do not know whether this advert was placed when Duveen purchased the house, but it is not unlikely. Whoever placed it also mentioned that omnibuses (horse-drawn in 1885) passed the house's entrance, and that by using them both the City and the West End were within 45 minutes' reach, which is roughly how long the journey lasts today.

Duveen' house, The Hawthorns, was purchased by the estate agent Ernest Owers, and demolished to create the row of shops (with flats and gables above them) standing on the southern corner of Golders Green Road and Finchley Road. This was already constructed and in full use before 1910, and has the intertwined letters 'E' and 'O' prominently displayed on the gable below which the offices of Ernest Owers used to be. The company was still there in the 1960s, when I was a child. Below this logo at number 1 Golders Green Road, there is currently a booking office for National Express coaches, many of which call at Golders Green station. Its neighbour to the west was an old-fashioned branch of Sainsbury's food store, in which I remember customers were served by shop assistants (rather than self-service). According to the architectural historian Nikolaus Pevsner (1902-1983), who lived near Golders Green in Hampstead's North End, this row of shops was completed in 1908. Duveen died in November that year. So, it is likely that The Hawthorns must have been sold and demolished soon before Duveen died.

Pam Fox wrote that the second Jewish person to move to Golders Green was Samuel Wolff. He was born in the East End and moved from West Ham to take up the job of the superintendent of the Jewish Cemetery, which was established in Hoop Lane in about 1896.

A great migration of Jewish people to Golders Green began soon after the Underground's extension arrived there in 1907. Some of them came from London's East End and others directly from Central and Eastern Europe. By 1917, there were between 200 and 250 Jewish families in the area. The first place of worship on high holidays was the hall of the Middlesex Auto-Car Company in West Heath Drive; it began to be used as such in 1913. The website of The Golders Green Synagogue (www.goldersgreenshul.org.uk/) related:

"The community has a long history dating back to 1915 when services were first held, during the First World War, in the hall of Golders Green Parish Church."

Like the Middlesex Auto-Car Company (no longer in existence), the parish hall is on West Heath Drive. A Jewish history website (www.jewishgen.org/jcr-uk/london/golders/history04_early_years.htm)

revealed that *both* the garage and the church hall had been used for services:

"The first record that religious services were held in the area was when the Community, with a congregation of 20 members, secured a temporary synagogue for the High Festivals in 1913. They used the hall of the Middlesex Auto-Car Company in West Heath Drive … The Community made arrangements with the Rev Herbert Trundle to use St Albans Church Hall, on North End Road for religious services. It was agreed that services were to be held on weekday mornings, Friday evenings, Saturday mornings and on Sunday mornings. The first service was held on Saturday 14th August 1915."

It was not until October 1921 when the foundation stone of the Golders Green Synagogue (on Dunstan Road) was laid. The synagogue, completed in 1922, was designed in a neo-classical (Georgian) style by Digby Lewis Solomon (1884-1962) and Joseph Messers. Various additions, designed by Ernest Joseph, were made by 1927. Later Ivor Warner designed other new parts, including a nursery. Solomon incorporated some then up-to-date steel construction features in his design (as noted in https://archive.jpr.org.uk/):

"A polite red brick neo-Georgian facade that blends in discreetly with the surrounding suburban houses in a neighbourhood that is still very popular with better-off London Jews. Yet it masks transitional building technology. Digby Solomon's (of Lewis Solomon & Son) original portion (1920-1) utilised steel construction but retained the column supports under the gallery…"

Carmelli Bagel Bakery
(Golders Green Road)

A kosher butcher and delicatessen on
Golders Green Road

Frieze on Eagle Lodge
(Golders Green Road)

Grodzinski's bakery on Golders Green Road

The presence of a synagogue in Golders Green probably stimulated further migration of Jewish people to the area. However, there was another reason for the arrival of Jewish people in Golders Green as Lynne Fertleman explained in an online article about the history of the Golders Green Synagogue (posted on www.jewishgen.org):

"One of the main reasons for the continued rise of Jewish immigration to the suburbs is that the Jews were still largely an immigrant population and the London County Council of 1923 had in force an anti-alien housing policy. This policy meant that only British citizens were eligible to accommodation on the council's housing estates. This approach was strengthened in 1925 when no alien was eligible for council housing even if they were paying rates. The areas of Golders Green, Finchley and Hendon were still in the County of Middlesex and were, therefore, not within the borders of the London County Council."

Fertleman also mentioned the initial difficulties that Jewish people faced when trying to obtain Kosher meat in Golders Green:

"The Jewish Chronicle had helped in the publicity in the community's requirements for a kosher butcher. In December 1917 there were approximately 200-250 families in the district. A butcher, E Barnett & Co Ltd of Aldgate, was approached in January 1919 to open a branch in Golders Green. However, Barnetts were not convinced that there were enough clientele to warrant opening a shop in Golders Green ... E Barnett & Co were prepared to deliver to the area if there was enough demand. However, there were still problems because they were unable to deliver in time for the meat to be properly koshered and cooked for the mid-day meal ... Finally, on 23rd January 1922 a long established butcher, J Nathan Limited, opened a kosher butcher at 22 North End Road."

With the growth of the Jewish population in Golders Green and nearby areas (including Hampstead Garden Suburb), new synagogues were opened including one at Alyth Gardens (in Temple Fortune) and in Norrice Lea (already described). Many more have been established after these. The extension of the Underground from Golders Green towards Hendon in 1923 and then to Edgware in 1924 led to the establishment of Jewish communities beyond Golders Green in Hendon and Edgware.

In addition to places of worship, Golders Green's shopping area began to be populated with many shops catering to Jewish gastronomic and religious requirements. Pam Fox described these in detail. Of these establishments, I can remember a few, such as Appenrodt's Delicatessen, where pickled gherkins were stored under pickling liquid in wooden barrels. My parents patronised this establishment. Another store we visited was Beecholme's Bakery, which was close to the bridge that carries the Northern Line tracks over Golders Green Road. It was run by Harry Steigman and his family, who were related to my father's sister's husband. What I did not know when I was a child was that a member of the Steigman family, Natty (the youngest of four brothers who helped their parents run the forerunner of Beecholme Bakeries) had volunteered to fight against Franco in the Spanish Civil War. Tragically, he was killed at the battle of Jarama (in February 1937) only two weeks after his arrival in Spain.

Although they were plenty of other 'Jewish' food shops, we did not patronise them because my family did not keep Kosher. Today, there is no shortage of shops and eateries offering Kosher and Israeli food. On a recent visit (2022), I noticed that the density of shops etcetera catering to the Jewish community along Golders Green Road increases significantly west of the railway bridge crossing it.

Throughout the 1930s, Jewish refugees from the Nazis came to England from Central Europe and Germany. Quite a few of them settled in Golders Green. Pam Fox related that many of these people came directly to northwest London, bypassing the traditional routes (e.g., via the East End) taken by earlier Jewish migrants. She mentioned that many of these arrivals already spoke English and some had family members in this country. They represented varying degrees of religiousness ranging from highly reformed (or even not observant) to deeply orthodox. Amongst these refugees was Hilda Wolfsfeld from Vienna. She commenced a business that was patronised by at least two female members of my family after they arrived in the Golders Green area in the 1950s. Her business was by then trading as 'Madame Leiberg', which was described as an "exclusive salon de corseterie". By the 1950s, this was then housed in a shop on the west side of Finchley Road very close to the Golders Green post office. Pam Fox noted that she was the chief competitor to Frank's lingerie outlet, also a Jewish business, on Golders Green Road.

As it passes through Golders Green, Finchley Road was, and still is, lined with buildings housing Jewish institutions including yeshivas, where young men receive religious training, and the Jewish Vegetarian Society (at number 855). The society was founded in 1960 and continues to thrive. Included in its premises, there is a restaurant that, according to a friend of mine, serves wonderful food, but at which a prior reservation is required. One establishment, which no longer exists, was at number 833 Finchley Road. Owned by Mr Frischwasser (a refugee from Nazi Germany), a highly observant Jewish man, it was the Freshwater Hostel for young Jewish men. The hostel was the temporary home for young Jewish men who had survived the concentration camps during the Holocaust and had been brought to England at the end of WW2. One of the hostel's residents, Kurt Klappholz (1927- 2000), was a close family friend and one of my father's colleagues at the London School of Economics ('LSE'). Martin Gilbert in his book about the young men rescued from the camps, "The Boys" (published in 1996), recorded that Kurt was in general happy at the hostel, but:

"In one respect, Kurt Klappholz was unhappy ... This was the attempt made to encourage greater religious worship."

Kurt remembered that there were about 15 residents in the hostel of which only 4 were orthodox. About half of the young men went to synagogue as encouraged, but, as Kurt recalled (quoted by Gilbert), he and some of his fellow residents did not welcome:

"… details of their lives dictated to them. In my own case, my stay at 833 Finchley Road led to my becoming more anti-religious and quite explicitly so, more than I had ever been in my life. Admittedly, previously my father was an atheist and certainly did not expect me to behave in a religious way."

Despite the unwanted pressuring to be religious, Kurt's stay at the hostel was beneficial as another survivor resident Eli Pfefferkorn described in his "The Musselmann at the Water Cooler" (publ. 2011):

"…the Freshwater Hostel was goal-oriented. By then it was assumed that we had bounced back to optimal levels of social norms and that the remaining psychological and other handicaps would straighten themselves out in the course of time. The hostel counsellors had a plan aimed at steering us to eventually become contributing members of society. After catching up on his elementary curriculum, my roommate Kurt Klappholz was among the first of us to attend high school. Other boys took up intensive studies guided by the hostel or attended vocational schools, and a few among us lingered in a twilight zone. I belonged to the last group."

Since WW2, Jewish life continues to be a significant feature in Golders Green's cultural tapestry. There are now about 40 synagogues (of varying sizes), other Jewish religious institutions, and about 30 Jewish schools in the area.

Some of Golders Green's former Jewish residents have moved to leafier districts further from central London, such as Edgware, Stanmore, and

Radlett. In their place, people from a wide range of ethnic backgrounds have moved in. Amongst these, the most significant (numerically) are people whose families originated in Korea, Japan, and the Indian subcontinent. According to the 2011 census for the Golders Green ward of the Borough of Barnet, within the population of about 21,500: 6975 described themselves as Jewish; 4913 as Christian; 2300 as Muslim; and 758 as either Hindu or Sikh. There also many people from Eastern Europe.

In recent times, Golders Green has become home to some ultra-orthodox Jewish sects ('Haredim'), as is also the case in northeast London's Stamford Hill. Every December, a large, tall, illuminated menorah is placed in the ground close to Golders Green station to celebrate the Jewish festival of Hannukah. This did not used to happen when I was a boy in the 1960s, and is just one of many signs of Golders Green's flourishing Orthodox community.

Antisemitism exists even in places where there are few or no Jewish people. Golders Green has had a substantial number of Jewish people for many decades, but until recently surprisingly little in the way of overt antisemitic activity. Pam Fox related that during the 1930s when Oswald Mosely and his Blackshirts were harassing Jewish folk in London's East End, things were better for Jews living in suburbs like Golders Green. She quoted a line published in a Jewish journal, "The Leader", in November 1938:

"While you play bridge in Golders Green, old people are living in the shadow of impending terror in Bethnal Green."

While the situation was far better in Golders Green at that time, the area has not been free from occasional antisemitic incidents. In 1947, during the founding of the state of Israel, there were a few antisemitic notices daubed on the windows of Jewish businesses in Golders Green. This was a short-lived interruption of the otherwise amicable relationship between Jewish people and their gentile neighbours, which existed ever since Jewish people began living in the area. In the 1950s and '60s, when I was a child, the only antisemitism I encountered in the early 1960s was from my best friend's parents, who lived across the road from the Jewish cemetery. In contrast, Pam Fox related that Peter Englander, who was a fellow pupil at the pre-preparatory school we attended in Finchley Road (in the late 1950s), told her that he felt very aware of being a member of a minority group. At that tender age, I did not feel the same.

A search of the internet for items about antisemitism in Golders Green revealed that there has been a marked increase in the frequency of incidents of an antisemitic nature in the area in recent years. For example, an article in the "Evening Standard" in May 2021 noted:

"Anti-Semitic attacks have increased by 500 per cent in two weeks as a London Rabbi said. Offenders were threatening to 'kill Jews' and rape their daughters ... 'For the first time, I told my children not to go out with their skullcaps on. I never thought I would tell my children to hide their Jewish identity,' the Rabbi, who wished to remain anonymous, said. 'We have not had cars driving through Jewish neighbourhoods shouting 'kill the Jews' before. They threatened to rape our daughters. We think they came down the M1 and deliberately drove through Jewish neighbourhoods in Golders Green, Finchley, and St John's Wood.'"

Well, let us hope things are not going to deteriorate further, especially now (2022) when the country is facing a dramatic economic downturn and there is continuing unrest in Israel. In any case, Jewish establishments like schools and synagogues now tend to be guarded by tough looking security personnel.

Until the present, on the whole relations between Golder Green's Jewish people and their gentile neighbours have been pretty good in an area that has been becoming increasingly cosmopolitan. Pam Fox noted that the ultra-orthodox communities tend to be more separatist than other folk in Golders Green. It is not inconceivable that their distinctive garb makes them an easy to identify as targets for those who harbour and/or exhibit antagonism towards Jewish people. Further, the ultra-orthodox tend to live in tightly knit communities, rather like self-imposed ghettos. This is a situation that has not existed in the UK since the Jews were expelled from Britain in early mediaeval times. The author of "Trials of the Diaspora. A History of Anti-Semitism in England", Anthony Julius, suggested that one reason for the relatively tolerant attitude of British gentiles towards the Jews over the centuries (since Oliver Cromwell allowed them back into the country) is that they have not lived in ghettos, as was the case in many places in mainland Europe. Instead, they have lived side-by-side with their gentile neighbours and have become more or less assimilated.

St Albans church hall, which also served briefly as a Jewish place of worship before about 1920

RECOLLECTING GOLDERS GREEN

One of my earliest memories is walking with my parents to the church hall next to St Albans Church in Golders Green to collect bottles of orange juice. The juice was delicious and richly flavoured. It was contained in large glass medicine bottles with cork stoppers and was supplied free of charge by the state during the 1950s. It was first provided by the state in 1941, and distributed to reduce the risk of vitamin C deficiency amongst young British children. In 1951, just before I was born, the Conservative Party won a General Election. Soon afterwards, the government restricted the supply of free orange juice to children under two years. My sibling was born in 1956, four years after me. Therefore, I must have been well under six years old when we made these trips to the church hall. Later, when I was at my pre-preparatory school and aged about 7, I had a small part in a play put on for pupils' parents in the church hall. We acted it on the small stage. I had a minor role as a magician.

Two shops in Golders Green particularly intrigued me when I was a little boy. One was an old-fashioned shop, Franks (established in 1928). It sold various clothing items, much of it was hosiery and lingerie. It was not the garments that interested me but the pneumatic system that was used to send money and receipts from the shop floor to an office somewhere above the shop. Money, bills, and receipts were placed in cylindrical capsules that were placed in tubes along which air was pumped to propel them from one part of the shop to another.

The other establishment was Importers (opened in 1928), a coffee retailer with a popular, old-fashioned café behind it. The front windows contained cylindrical coffee roasters, which could be seen from the street. The cylinders were made with fine metal meshwork. Filled with coffee beans, they rotated slowly above gas burners. The air inside the shop was filled with a wonderful aroma that must have helped sell the coffee beans and powders stocked on the shelves of the shop and in open topped sacks on the floor. We used to pass this shop often, but rarely entered it because my mother preferred to buy coffee at the Algerian Coffee Store, which still exists in Old Compton Street in Soho. Despite this, I always stopped to watch the roasters rotating and savour the odour of the coffee whenever I passed that shop.

I am too young to have seen trams running on Finchley Road because they had stopped operating in 1936. I do remember watching the double-decker trolleybuses that replaced them. Their route numbers began with '6' (e.g., the 660 ran from North Finchley to Hammersmith via Golders Green. The 645 also ran along Finchley Road on its way from Barnet to Canons Park). They travelled almost noiselessly past my pre-preparatory school, Golders Hill School (see later). I remember that inside the (now disused) Finchley Road entrance to Golders Green station, there was a machine (housed in a large wooden box) that contained a large diameter circular sheet of paper. Whenever a trolleybus passed a certain place, a device in the machine made a short black line on the disc. In early 1962, the trolleybuses ceased operating and were replaced by motor buses.

During the last three months of 1963, we lived in Chicago, Illinois. There, we experienced and enjoyed self-service supermarkets for the first time. So, I was excited when the first supermarket opened in Golders Green soon after we arrived back from the USA. I cannot accurately recall the supermarket's original name (it might have been Premier or Premium), but soon it was called Mac Market, when it was taken over by the Mac Fisheries Company. Prior to the opening of the supermarket, food stores, including the old Mac Fishery on Golders Green Road and Sainsbury's at the eastern end of that road (close to the clock tower), were not self-service: one queued up to be served by shopkeepers standing behind counters laden with food items. If you wanted a product, butter for example, the assistant cut the amount you required, weighed it, and wrapped it up.

The supermarket occupied a plot on the corner of Golders Green Road and a small service road called Broadwalk Lane on which there used to be a small pet shop (the space it occupied has now been bricked-up). Years later, the building that housed Mac Market was occupied by a newer supermarket (Country Market) that stocked many Kosher and Israeli products. Currently, a branch of Tesco's occupies the site of Golders Green's first ever supermarket. Just east of the supermarket, there is a wonderful Jewish bakery, Carmelli's (established in 1987). This large bakery sells a wide variety of Kosher breads and cakes. Beyond its counters, the busy kitchen at the rear of the shop can be seen.

Between 1965 and 2010, when it closed, there was a branch of the famous East End Kosher restaurant, Blooms, on Golders Green Road, not far from Carmelli's. This popular eatery served Ashkenazi Jewish cuisine. The few times I ate there, I was unimpressed by both its food and the staff who served it. As the food critic Giles Coren once noted, Ashkenazi food is like Polish food without pork and cream. I prefer the Sephardic and Israeli cuisine, which used to be served at Solly's. This place was on the first floor of the building adjoining the former Woolworths shop (see below). It closed in 2014, having opened 24 years earlier. As the "Jewish Chronicle" noted in its edition published on the 6th of June 2014:

"Now the shwarma towers have turned for the last time as one of London's first kosher Israeli restaurants closed this week, prompting laments from loyal customers … Pop culture journalist Chas Newkey Burden described the news as 'shwarmaggedon'."

The article also reported:

"When Solly's opened, barely a handful of kosher restaurants existed in Golders Green Road, including Bloom's, which bit the dust in 2010 … Now in a 200-metre stretch at the station end of Golders Green Road, there are 11 kosher supervised restaurants and cafes, six others, like Solly's, licensed by the LDB. While Ms Sade would not criticise the rabbinic authorities, she believed the number of kosher restaurants in such a small area 'ridiculous'."

Another supermarket built far later than the one described above, a branch of Sainsburys, occupies the site of the Ionic, one of Golders Green's two former cinemas, both of which I frequented in my childhood. The other cinema, long since demolished, was the ABC that stood on Golders Green Road northwest of the main shopping area at the end of Ambrose Avenue. I watched several films there.

Woolworths, which was located on Golders Green Road next to the public library, figures amongst my childhood recollections. This old-fashioned store, a magnificent emporium, stocked everything from plant bulbs to lightbulbs, from liquorice to lawnmowers. Its plaster ceiling was decorated with an elaborate stuccoed pattern. Although illuminated with electric lamps, some of the shop's old-fashioned gas lamps still hung from the ceiling. They had little chains dangling from them to regulate the gas flow. Shoppers were assisted by salespersons: it was not a self-service store. Oddly, I have no memory of the shop after its modernisation in 1971. By comparing old with recent photographs, although the ground floor of the building has been remodelled, the appearance of the façade at the first-floor level and the pediment above it remain the same as it was when Woolworths occupied it.

My parents loved Italians, Italy, and espresso coffee. During my early childhood, there were plenty of coffee bars but finding one whose coffee met my exacting parents' approval was difficult. One place, which gained my parents' custom during the 1950s, was the Bamboo Bar on Finchley

Road in Golders Green. It was located under the Northern Line bridge which straddles Finchley Road close to Golders Green station, and opposite the now disused entrance to the station. The walls of the Bamboo Bar were lined with bamboo. It was run by two Italian men, Lorenzo Fraquelli and Simone Lavarini. My parents enjoyed chatting with these fellows. In 1955, they opened the first branch of what was to become the now large chain of Spaghetti Houses. The Bamboo Bar closed long ago. It is now part of a popular Italian restaurant called Artista.

A cousin, who was born in 1955 and lived in Hampstead Garden Suburb, recalled that in the 1960s, the shops in Golders Green Road were quite 'upmarket' (e.g., Russell & Bromley, Lilley & Skinner, Franks, Weiss, and Jaegers) compared to what is there now. This reminded me that once, probably in the early 1970s, I bought a scarf for the young lady who has become my wife, in the Golders Green Road branch of Jaeger's, which is no longer in existence. An article in the "Ham and High" newspaper dated November 2008 (and updated in February 2020) confirms what my cousin told me. It related:
"During the 1966 World Cup, the WAGS of the England football team came to do their shopping on Golders Green Road. At that time the high street had plush shops and boutiques aplenty, the remnants of which were visible until about 10 years ago.
Russell & Bromley, Bally, Jaeger and Benetton are just a few of the big brand names that were on the high street. Now Golders Green has become a street with lots of Polish shops, Jewish shops, charity shops, coffee

shops and not a lot else. And the general estimation in which the locals hold the street seems to have plummeted and is providing dark times for owners too."

Although I remember Jaeger's, I have no other recollection of Golders Green Road being rich in smart shops. My mother, who did most of our family's shopping, only bought essentials in Golders Green; she preferred shopping in the West End. Once during the 1960s when the anti-apartheid campaigners tried to discourage people from buying goods imported from South Africa, she overheard the following conversation in a fruiterer's shop in Golders Green Road. A woman had taken some oranges to be weighed by the salesman. She asked:

"Are these oranges from South Africa?"

"No, Madame."

My South African born mother mischievously asked the lady what was wrong with South African oranges. The answer she was given by the woman shocked her:

"I wouldn't buy oranges from South Africa because they might have been touched by black people."

L'Artista restaurant on Finchley Road.
The former Bamboo Bar occupied the left half of this building beneath the Northern Line tracks

Gothic Cottages on Highfield Road

The White Swan pub (now demolished) in 2017

Machzide Hadath synagogue

BRENT BRIDGE TO THE STATION

Prior to the arrival of the Underground, Golders Green consisted mainly of a series of well-separated, mostly large houses running alongside what is now Golders Green Road between Brent Bridge and the common land on which the station was constructed in the first years of the 20th century. Most of these dwellings were between the bridge and Hoop Lane. We will now explore this stretch of road.

Near Brent Bridge, there is a pedestrian bridge with elegant spiral approach ramps crossing the North Circular Road. This highway that runs for part of its way in the valley of the Brent, was open for traffic by the 1930s. Since then, it has been improved in places. It would be an excellent throughway were it not for bottlenecks where it narrows near both Ealing and Southgate. Ascending the steep slope of Golders Green Road, we reach a small group of Victorian cottages that stand on Highfield Road next to Caroline Court, an undistinguished looking block of flats. One of the cottages bears the nameplate '1 Gothic Cottages'. They appear on a detailed map surveyed in 1893/4. So, they are among the oldest surviving man-made features in Golders Green.

A newer building on Highfield Road is one of the area's many synagogues: Machzike Hadath (meaning 'upholders of the law'), whose history is well described on a website (www.machzikehadath.com). Its mainly Eastern European congregation was founded in 1891, when it was based in the East End. In 1898, it began worshipping in a building, formerly a Christian chapel, on the corner of Fournier Street and Brick Lane (in what is now the Brick Lane Mosque). In 1951, a branch of the synagogue opened at 215 Golders Green Road in the home of a rabbi. As the Jewish population began to decline in the East End, this suburban branch became the new Machzike Hadath Synagogue. The present custom-built synagogue on Highfield Road was ready for use in 1983.

The White Swan pub stood on the west side of Golders Green Road (at number 243) almost opposite the start of Highfield Road. On a detailed map surveyed in the 1890s, there was also a pub was marked on the east side of the road. This was the Prince Albert (290 Golders Green Road), which was near a line of cottages called 'Albert Row', which no longer existed by the mid-1930s. It was located between Woodlands and Princes Park Avenue. The Prince Albert closed, and was demolished in the 1990s. I have vague memories of this hostelry with its fake half-timbering that stood slightly above the road.

The White Swan had been in existence since 1826 or earlier. Howitt noted that this hostelry was:

"… the last house of call before crossing the narrow bridge across the River Brent beyond which the road rises to the village of Hendon."

In his book, there is a photograph of the pub, showing that it was an irregularly shaped edifice whose exterior was covered with overlapping wooden planks (clapboard). I last saw the pub in 2017, when I took a photograph of it. By then, it had been rebuilt and no longer remotely resembled the image in Howitt's book. It was fortunate that I took the photograph because by then it had been closed for four years. It was demolished in 2018, and now a small block of flats, appropriately named Swan Court, stands where people used to enjoy taking refreshment.

Between Highfield Road and Russell Gardens, Golders Green Road is lined with shops, many of them catering to members of the Jewish community whose dietary preferences are for strictly Kosher foodstuff. These shops include Kosher Kingdom and Menachem's Glatt Kosher Butcher and Delicatessen. The latter stands on the corner of Alba Gardens, whose name recalls the now demolished Alba Lodge that used to stand in the neighbourhood. A branch of Grodzinski's (Kosher) bakeries, now renamed 'Grodz', is located almost opposite Kosher Kingdom. Founded in the East End by Harris and Judith Grodzinski, migrants from Varanova (now in Belarus) in the Russian Empire who arrived in England in about 1888, the company grew and established branches all over London, and it has two branches in Toronto (Canada). My parents used to buy rye bread from the branches in the centre of Golders Green and in Temple Fortune.

The Maurice and Vivien Wohl Campus

Double-headed eagle on the facade of Eagle Lodge

Heading onwards towards the Underground station, we pass a modern building, which is remarkably elegant compared with the structures surrounding it: the Maurice and Vivienne Wohl Campus. Son of a rabbi, Maurice Wohl (1917-2007) was born in the East End, of Eastern European parents. He became a property developer, forming his United Real Property Trust in 1948. He became prosperous by building office buildings in parts of London damaged during WW2. He was a generous philanthropist, donating money for the construction of worthy foundations both in the UK and Israel. Just before his wife Vivienne died of cancer, aged 59 in 2005, the couple founded Maurice and Vivienne Wohl Philanthropic Foundation. The Campus in Golders Green Road was funded by this, and serves as a Jewish community centre for the care of the elderly and those in need. It includes (according to www.wohl.org.uk): "… a 54-bed nursing and dementia care home with six dedicated respite beds and 45 independent living apartments. The community centre is situated in the heart of the community and invites in the wider public, with a range of social and therapeutic activities, a multi media library and computer suite, kosher restaurants, a hairdresser and a landscaped courtyard."

About 350 yards southeast of the Wohl Campus and opposite the King Solomon Hotel, there stands a large block of flats called Eagle Lodge. Before discussing this, I will mention the currently named Sage Nursing Home on the corner of Ambrose Avenue. This was built on the site of a cinema that was part of the ABC chain in my childhood. Opened as 'The Lido Picture House' in 1928, it was demolished some years ago.

Eagle Lodge has some neo-classical sculptural friezes and a magnificent, wide two-storey high archway - the entrance to a courtyard flanked by other blocks belonging to this housing complex. High above the building's pediments, there are bas-reliefs depicting double-headed eagles. As this mythological creature interests me, I will go into some detail about this block and Russian presence in Golders Green.

According to Pam Fox, Eagle Lodge was one of several mansion blocks built on the sites of former large villas with extensive grounds that used to line Golders Green Road. She wrote that:

"It was designed by a Polish architect who carved the Polish eagle onto its façade, giving the block its name."

Eagle Lodge was bombed during the Blitz, and amongst the fatalities was a woman who had been a Russian Princess.

Although I doubt that Ms Fox's book attracts many Polish nationalist readers, her note about the eagle might upset them. The Polish eagle used heraldically or as a symbol has only one head. Having been subjected to domination by the Russians for many years, to confuse the single-headed eagle of Poland with the double-headed version used by their Russian neighbours might not go down too well with Poles.

As for the "Polish architect", there is another problem. Eagle Lodge was, according to the architectural historian Nikolaus Pevsner, designed by MV Braikevitch and built 1935-37. Mikhail Vasilievich Braikevitch (1874-1940) was a Russian engineer and art collector born in (the)

Ukraine. A pamphlet published by the London Borough of Barnet (which contains the district of Golders Green), "The 1917 Revolution & Barnet's Russian Heritage", noted:

"Possibly the most interesting Russian resident was Mikhail Vladimirovitch Braikevitch of Woodstock Avenue. He had been an important engineer in the construction of the Trans-Siberian Railway, was the mayor of Odessa before the war, and had been a member of the interim government, who ran Russia between February 1917 and the October Revolution. Remarkable as all these things are, it was his art collection which was most important. Having settled in England, he started to collect works of art smuggled out of Russia from fellow refugees … and amassed one of the best collections of Russian art outside of Russia itself. On his death in 1940, he left the collection to the Ashmolean Museum in Oxford, but we can imagine an ordinary house in Golders Green with some of the greatest works of Russian art on the walls."

It was at Braikevitch's suggestion and following a visit to his home in Golders Green that the remarkable Russian composer Nicolas Medtner (1880-1951), a contemporary of Rachmaninov and Scriabin, shifted from Paris to London in 1935. The composer and his family settled into a new home on Wentworth Road in Golders Green. He lived at number 62 until his death. Braikevitch lived in Golders Green's Woodstock Avenue.

The above-mentioned pamphlet revealed that Russians began residing in Golders Green before WW1:

"The best known is the dancer Anna Pavlova, who lived in Ivy House in North End Road between 1912 and her death in 1931 … Most were

Russians Jews who had escaped the infamous Tsarist Pogroms of the 1880s. They settled in the East End and Soho, and by the 1900s had done well enough to move from Bethnal Green and Soho to what was, from 1907 to 1923, the end of the underground line and a healthier part of London. Interesting as they are, their children considered themselves more English than Russian and identified with a cosmopolitan diaspora of which Russia was only a part. For example, when the area received many Jewish refugees from the Nazi persecution of the 1930s, Golders Green library found that it did not have enough German language stock to meet demand (the Chief Librarian noting in 1936 that German had replaced French in demand for foreign language books almost overnight.) Bruno Meyer, whose family had been in Russia for more than 300 years before he came to Golders Green in 1910, stepped forward with a donation of 300 German books from his own library."

It added that after the Russian Revolution of 1917:

"With its 'European' feel, Golders Green was more comfortable to these new refugees escaping from the Bolshevik Russia than other parts of London. ... Ironically, the Bolsheviks had an embassy house in the Hampstead Garden Suburb in Bigwood Road. In September 1918, at a time when the Russians had made peace with the Germans but Britain was still at war, armed police raided the address and the Bolshevik ambassador, Maxim Litvinoff, was taken off to Brixton gaol along with two of his aids. Later, the NKVD (precursor to the KGB) had a training manual in the 1930s for its spies which recommended that the bandstand in Hendon Park was a good location for secret meetings, because foreigners did not attract quite so much attention in Hendon."

Litvinoff's (i.e., Litvinov's) Russian People's Embassy was housed for a few months at number 11 Bigwood Road. He and his wife Ivy had moved there from West Hampstead. Golders Green and Temple Fortune were also home to the Russian violinist Minna Tomchinski (she flourished as a concert musician in the 1920s), and the ballerina Mademoiselle Nicolaeva (maybe, Nadine Nicolaeva-Legat [1889-1971]). The Count Vladimir Kleinmichel (1901-1982) and his wife the Countess Marie (1893-1979; née von Carlow) lived in Woodstock Avenue until the 1950s.

Moving on from Eagle Lodge, we arrive at Golders Green Library (opened in 1935) near the corner of Ravenscroft Avenue. This brick building with white masonry trimmings was one of my favourite local haunts during my childhood. It had a large children's library. When I was old enough (maybe about 12), the library's regulations permitted me to access the larger adults' library. It was here that an excellent selection of books about the Nazi Holocaust were kept on open-access shelves. From these, I gained an early, detailed knowledge of the horrors of this dreadful era. Recently (2022), I revisited the library. The room which used to house the children's library in my childhood has now been rented out to a Jewish organization that now uses it as a Chabad house (a place for disseminating a version of traditional Judaism as practised by members of the Chabad-Lubavitch belief group). The former Woolworth shop was to the right of the library when viewed from Golders Green Road.

A few yards southeast of the library on the corner of Golders Green Road and a small service road called Broadwalk Lane, there is a branch of Tesco's. It stands on the site of Golders Green's first ever supermarket (see above).

Facing it (across Golders Green Road) is a gothic revival style church. It has been used by a Greek Orthodox (Christian) congregation since 1968. Now the Greek Orthodox Cathedral of the Holy Cross & St. Michael, it was constructed as the Church of England's 'St Michael's Church' in 1914 (to the design of JT Lee). A clock tower, surmounted by a delicate cupola supported by thin columns, was added to the church in 1960. On one of its walls, there is a bas-relief of St Michael with one foot on a serpent. On the northeast corner of the church, there is a plaque listing people who died in WW1. Near this, there is a crucifix standing in the garden next to the church. Its design, typical of C of E crucifixes, predates the arrival of the Greek congregation.

Golders Green public library

Greek Orthodox Cathedral of
Holy Cross and St Michael
(Golders Green Road)

Greek Orthodox Cathedral of the Holy Cross and St Michael
(Golders Green Road)

Although the interior of the church maintains some of its original C of E fittings, such as its stained-glass windows, the font designed in a mock mediaeval style, and some wall mounted memorials in English, a great deal of effort has been made to create the atmosphere of a Greek Orthodox place of worship. The walls of the side aisles have been painted with religious scenes. There is a decorated iconostasis and several framed icons. Elaborate chandeliers hang above the nave. Despite the additional fittings to convert the church for Greek Orthodox worship, the original gothic revival features of the building's interior are evident, but harmonise well with the later additions. A bridge carrying the Northern line obliquely across Golders Green Road is a few yards southeast of the church. Beecholme's Bakery (see above) was close to its western end, but east of it.

Between the library and the station, there are many shops and eateries, many of which cater to Kosher customers and those who enjoy Middle Eastern cuisine, such as can be found in Israel. During my adolescence and early adulthood, there used to be two Chinese restaurants on this stretch of the road: The Water Margin, and one closer to the station, which my father and I preferred. These have gone, but today (2022), Met Su Yan, a pan-Asian eatery on Golders Green Road serves "… authentic fusion foods serving exquisite dishes using the freshest produce prepared for the highest Kashrus standards, and all meat is Glatt Kosher." Today, there is a much wider range of cuisines available along Golders Green Road than there was when I was in my teens. In addition to Chinese and Israeli restaurants, there are now also establishments offering Japanese, Korean, Persian, and Turkish food.

The western end of Hoop Lane (see later) meets the main road. This side road, which heads towards the Hampstead Garden Suburb, was probably named after a pub, The Hoop, which has long-since disappeared. According to a detailed 18th century map (www.bada.org/object/estates-and-farms-golders-green) of fields and farms, this was 'The Cock in Hoop Ale House) located opposite the start of what was then 'Weild Lane' (leading to 'Weild Hatch'), and is now Hoop Lane. The pub was closed in 1896 after it was discovered that the owner had been dead for many years. Hodford Road (named after the former Hodford Farm), where the poet Dannie Abse (1923-2014) lived from about 1957, leads southwest from Golders Green Road to Rodborough Road. At the corner where they meet at an acute angle, stands Trinity Church, a Methodist and United Reform place of worship. Built in 1922 to the designs of George E Withers, it has four towers topped with copper domes, and many features borrowed from Byzantine and Romanesque architecture.

Trinity Methodist Church

South side of the east end of Golders Green Road (built by 1910)

1930's finger post on Finchley Road next to Golders Green station

Curved Neo-classical bank facade to the right of the shop designed by Erno Goldfinger

Number 2 Golders Green Road is a fine example of 20th century modernism. Built originally as Weiss's upmarket lingerie shop and completed in 1935, it was designed by the Hungarian born architect Ernő Goldfinger (1902-1987). Since it was built, this building, with some curved glass windows, has served a variety of purposes. Now (2022), its ground floor is occupied by a bank and the floor above by a dental clinic. This modernistic building is next (west of) to an edifice on the corner of Finchley Road: bank premises built in 1911 with an elegant curved neo-classical façade in white Portland stone with pillars topped with Ionic capitals.

This brings us to the eastern end of Golders Green Road and its intersection with Finchley Road. A flat-topped clock tower stands in a triangular area where Golders Green Road meets Finchley Road and North End Road. Made of whitish Portland stone, it is square in cross-section and bears four blue clocks with gold-coloured Roman numerals, one near the top of each of its four sides. The words 'Loyalty', 'Justice', 'Courage', and 'Honour' are inscribed on blocks above the clocks. Possibly designed by Frank T Dear, this was erected as a war memorial in 1923 after WW1. It is like a war memorial that Dear designed in south London's Stockwell. Next to the base of the north side of the tower there is a metal plaque and a metal replica of an open book: they record the names of Golders Green people who died in WW1 and WW2 respectively. The words "Their Names Liveth For Evermore' are inscribed near the base of one of the sides of the tower. The monument reminds me of a similar-looking but shorter WW1 memorial I have seen in central Bangalore (India).

Before the arrival of the Underground in 1907, where the war memorial now stands was in the middle of fields. Then, most of Golders Green was further west along Golders Green Road. Now, the clock tower has become the centre of modern Golders Green. At the corner of Finchley Road and the western end of North End Road, there is an old-fashioned finger post: one arrow is marked 'Hampstead', another 'Finchley', and the third 'London'. That the latter, which points south towards Swiss Cottage, is marked 'London' rather than another part of the city such as Swiss Cottage, suggests to me that the sign dates to a time when Golders Green was not considered part of London. A document on the barnet.moderngov.co.uk suggested it was put in place in about 1935. This was while Golders Green was still part of the County of Middlesex, rather than part of London. An old photograph of this spot taken before the Underground had arrived at Golders Green shows that there was a finger post on this corner, but not the same one as now. And Evelyn Waugh, who was a child in Golders Green, and less than 4 years old before 1907, recalled that around that time there was a similar signpost at that spot. He recalled (many decades later) that its 'arms' pointed towards 'Hampstead', 'Hendon', and 'London'.

ONCE A COUNTRY TRACK: HOOP LANE

Hoop Lane runs between Golders Green Road and Hampstead Garden Suburb. As I have described it in detail in my book "Beneath a Wide Sky: Hampstead and its Environs", here is a briefer account of the lane's attractions.

Appearing on a map published in 1760, Hoop Lane is one of the oldest thoroughfares in Golders Green. Along its course, it crosses Finchley Road (see later). Southwest of Finchley Road, Hoop Lane was devoid of buildings as late as 1897. Near where the Lane met Golders Green Road, there was a building set in the middle of a large plot: The Oaks. This property had disappeared by 1920. Between Golders Green Road and the railway bridge crossing Hoop Lane, there is a building with neo-classical features and a tall brick vehicle entry arch. This used to be the Golders Green telephone exchange. There are proposals to redevelop it (and the courtyard it encloses) as a communal or commercial centre. By 1912, there were plant nursery buildings on Hoop Lane. The nurseries have been replaced with housing. A building, now the Oyo Central Hotel, stands where Hoop Lane meets Finchley Road. This is the oldest surviving 20th century building in Golders Green. Another early building (now Glentree estate agent) stands opposite it on the east side of Finchley Road. It is close to where the Roman Catholic Church of Edward the Confessor stands today. This church was completed by October 1915.

My earliest memories of Hoop Lane date to when I was three or four years old. At that age, I attended a kindergarten in Hoop Lane. This was in the hall attached to Golders Green's Unitarian Church (designed in the 'Byzantine revival' style by the architects Reginald Farrow and Sydney R Turner, and opened in 1925). The church contains artworks including a mural by Ivon Hitchens (1893-1979). The kindergarten was under the direction of 'Miss' Schreuer, who lived a few doors away in Hoop Lane. I never knew much about her, and I am not sure what became of her, but I heard rumours that the end of her life was not a happy one. Today, the hall, where her school flourished, is a Montessori kindergarten.

On the north-eastern corner of Finchley Road's intersection with Hoop Lane, there stands a shop. For at least forty years, it has been the premises of Glentree International, an estate agent. Before that, it was a dairy shop with a triangular floor plan run by the Express Dairy company. Its counter was at the shortest end of the shop opposite its entrance, which was at the apex of the triangle. Next to it, accessible from Hoop Lane, the company had a depot for re-charging and re-stocking its electric milk delivery floats.

Most of Hoop Lane to the east of Finchley Road is dedicated to the deceased. On the northern side of the road, there is a spacious Jewish cemetery, an undulating sea of gravestones on gently sloping ground. On the southern side, stands the Golders Green Crematorium.

The crematorium was opened in 1902 by Sir Henry Thompson (1720-1904), founder and president of the Cremation Society of Great Britain established in 1874. Its buildings are all close to the tall brick boundary wall that runs along Hoop Lane. Behind them spread attractive and extensive landscaped memorial gardens. According to www.historicengland.org.uk website, the main buildings were designed in the 'Romanesque Lombardic style'. They present a forbidding appearance. Many of the original buildings were designed by teams that included Alfred Yeates (1867-1944) and Ernest George (1839-1922), who was cremated at Hoop Lane. They formed a business partnership in 1892. George's speciality was garden architecture. The gardens and some of the buildings at the crematorium are fine examples of his work. Although the various buildings exhibit a certain architectural homogeneity, they were built over several decades as, gradually, money became available to pay for their construction.

It is worth visiting the inside of the Ernest George Columbarium. This building houses urns (containing ashes) and memorials. Amongst the incinerated remains in this columbarium are those of Sigmund Freud and his wife, as well as Anna Pavlova, the ballet dancer. Many other famous people have been cremated at this crematorium. These include, to name but a very few, Ivor Novello, Bram Stoker, Peter Sellers, Ronnie Scott, Ernő Goldfinger, Kingsley Amis, Enid Blyton, Rudyard Kipling, and Ernest Bevin.

Not all the ashes of the cremated are stored or scattered in the Crematorium's grounds. Some have been taken away to be disposed of elsewhere, as were, for example, the ashes of Soviet politician and a proposer of the idea of Lenin's tomb in Moscow, Leonid Krasin (1870-1926). His ashes were buried in the Kremlin Wall Necropolis.

Another Communist, Harry Pollitt (1890-1960), was cremated at Golders Green. A crowd of 5000 party comrades swarmed through the streets of north London to attend the funeral. They were led by the singer Paul Robeson (1898-1976). It must have been quite an occasion. According to an account in "The Nevada Herald" (10th of July 1960):

"… Many in the crowd brandished Red flags as successive speakers mounted the pulpit in the crematorium chapel to give funeral orations. Between tributes, Robeson sung 'Joe Hill' and 'England Arise'"

Having seen the largest of the chapels several times, most of the 5000 would have had to wait outside it. For those who are interested, there are a couple of short newsreel films showing the funeral procession passing through Golders Green and up Hoop Lane to the crematorium: they can be watched online.

My mother was one of many thousands to have been cremated in Golders Green. She was a sculptress. Other artists cremated here included, to mention a few, Boris Anrep, Walter Crane, Edwin Lutyens, and Percy Wyndham Lewis. Hindus, who often prefer that their corpses are cremated, frequently make use of the services of the crematorium. However, I knew nothing of these matters during the many journeys that I made by foot along Hoop Lane during my younger years, when my mind was focussed on the future rather than the past.

There is a poem, "Death Wish" written by Spike Milligan (1918-2002) in 1944. It begins:

"Bury me anywhere,

Somewhere near a tree …"

It ends:

"But please -

don't bury me

In Golders Green."

In some versions, including one recording of Milligan reciting it, the poem ends with the words: "… don't burn me in Golders Green." What he had against Golders Green (or its crematorium or cremation) is unclear to me. He was buried at Winchelsea in Sussex.

The Jewish Cemetery in Hoop Lane is divided into two sections. The western half contains mostly upright gravestones, and the eastern, mainly horizontal gravestones. The vertical headstones are characteristic of the Ashkenazi tradition, and the horizontal of the Sephardic. A book, "A History in our Time - Rabbis and Teachers Buried at Hoop Lane Cemetery" (published by the Leo Baeck College in 2006), provides a history of the cemetery. It opened for 'business' in about 1896. The juxtaposition of the graves of these two Jewish communities in the same burial ground is unusual. "The Jewish Yearbook" for the year 5658 (Jewish calendar; 1897 AD) noted of the cemetery:

"… a new cemetery at Golders'-green was also made ready for its melancholy purpose this last year. This cemetery has the curious distinction of being used by both the Orthodox Sephardim and the Reform Congregation of the West London Synagogue of British Jews."

The reason for this juxtaposition was that the two separate Jewish communities had bought neighbouring plots of land. Many years after the purchases, some of the land was sold for house building on Temple Fortune Lane (this happened in 1973, and includes the estate on Sheridan Walk), and another part to build a synagogue, the North Western Reform Synagogue (built in 1936) on Alyth Gardens.

The cemetery contains graves of many notable people including that of Dr Leo Baeck (1873-1956), who was born in Germany and became a leader in both Liberal and Progressive Judaism. During WW2, he represented all German Jews and narrowly avoided being murdered at Theresienstadt. More recently, another well-known Ashkenazi, Rabbi Hugo Gryn (1930 - 1996), a cleric and a broadcaster, was buried here. Amongst those who are buried in the Sephardi section, one is of particular interest to me. This is the barrister and historian Philip Guedalla (1889-1944), who was related to my late mother's family, albeit quite distantly.

Hoop Lane is one of the 'gateways' to Hampstead Garden Suburb, an area I will discuss further on in this text.

The letters E and O intertwined on a gable above number 1 Golders Green Road mark the building occupied from about 1908 by the estate agents Ernest Owers

Belvedere Court designed by Ernst Freud

A GOLDERS GREEN VIGNETTE

During the late 1990s, our then young daughter had a baby-sitter called Bridie. Although Bridie was already well into her eighties when we first met her, she was a remarkably sprightly lady. Born in a rural part of the west of Ireland, she came to England in her late teens. On arrival in England, she and her husband were cared for by the Salvation Army in exchange for taking a pledge never to drink alcohol again. Bridie never reneged on this promise. To earn a living in London, where she settled, she became a domestic servant. Hearing that I had been brought up in Golders Green, she told me the following story.

Sometime before WW2, Bridie was employed as a maid in a Jewish household in Golders Green. She looked after the family's children and carried out many household duties. Even though it was not a particularly wealthy family, Bridie recalled that she wore uniforms when on duty. There was one outfit that she wore in daytime and in the evening, she changed into another. As she did with our daughter, Bridie became fond of the family's two young sons.

Many years later, when Bridie had become a grandmother and our daughter's baby-sitter, she used to spend her spare time travelling around London by bus (making use of her old age free bus pass). One day, she was waiting for a bus at the stop closest to Golders Green's Sainsbury's (on the site of the Ionic cinema), when a well-dressed late middle-aged man in the queue said to her:

"Goodness! Is it you, Bridie? We have not seen each other for so many years."

After a moment, Bridie realised that she was being addressed by one of the two boys, whom she had looked after in the house in Golders Green before the War. Just then, a bus arrived, and as her former charge was about to embark, he shouted:

"This is my bus. Are you taking it, Bridie?"

Bridie misheard what he had said, and by the time she realised, the bus had pulled away, leaving her at the bus stop. She told me that if she had known he was taking that bus, she would have joined him. As far as I know, she has never seen him again.

FROM CHILDS HILL TO TEMPLE FORTUNE

Finchley Road was completed in 1835. It was originally a toll road (a 'turnpike') from the West End to Finchley with toll collection points at Swiss Cottage and Childs Hill, both south of Golders Green. It was laid out as an alternative to an older, far steeper route, which crossed the steep hills of Hampstead, on its way between central London and both Finchley and Hendon. Despite Finchley Road being used by regular stagecoach services, and later (in the 1890s) by horse-drawn omnibuses, Golders Green only began to be extensively developed after the Underground arrived in 1907.

Childs Hill (about 259 feet above sea level) already had that name in 1593. However, there has been a settlement at this location since early mediaeval times (or earlier). There was a long-established pub, The Castle, at Childs Hill until about 2016. It was on the corner of Finchley Road and Hermitage Lane, until it was demolished to make room for a new block of flats. The new block of flats bears a commemorative plaque celebrating the fact that near it there was a toll gate, which was abolished in 1871 when Finchley Road ceased being a toll road. The barnet.gov.uk website related that at Childs Hill by the 1870s:

"… a number of laundries at Childs Hill cleaned clothes for people in the new suburbs of West London and Hampstead. Clothes washed in London were thought to be susceptible to waterborne disease, such as cholera and typhoid, and Child's Hill, then still in the countryside, was supplied by a series of small streams coming off Hampstead Heath."

Between Childs Hill and Golders Green, there used to be a ten-pin bowling alley. I do not know when it was demolished, but I remember going there with school friends in the late 1960s. Prior to becoming a bowling alley, the building had housed a skating rink, and then a cinema (The Regal, which opened in 1929).

Before reaching Golders Green, Finchley Road passes the site of a now demolished gothic revival church building, which stood near to Helenslea Avenue. Formerly the Presbyterian Church of St Ninian, it was built in 1911 to the designs of T Phillip Figgis (1858-1948), who also designed some Northern Line London Underground stations (e.g., the domed Kennington station). In 1982, the church became the home of the (Hindu) Shree Swaminarayan Temple. By 2009, its congregation had grown so much that the congregation moved to a new site in Harrow. The church/temple has been replaced by a dull-looking block of flats (849 Finchley Road).

Just south of the Golders Green war memorial, outside number 604 Finchley Road, there is an old metal milestone placed by 'Hendon Parish'. It records that Regents Park is 3 miles in one direction and Barnet is 6 ¼ miles in the other. The historicengland.org.uk website noted that this marker was manufactured and placed in position about 1830. It stands almost facing the building housing The Jewish Vegetarian Society (see above), across the main road.

On the east side of Finchley Road, about 55 yards north of the old milestone and set back from the road, there is a branch of Sainsbury's supermarket chain. This non-descript building stands on the site once occupied by a far grander edifice: The Ionic Cinema. With Ionic pillars supporting a triangular pediment with a centrally located circular window, this picture-house was designed by Major WJ King, and opened in 1911. Its opening ceremony was attended by the ballerina Anna Pavlova, who had her home next to the North End Road entrance to Golders Hill Park. A website (cinematreasures.org) noted:

"Inside the auditorium, there was a barrel ceiling and a horse-shoe shaped balcony, which had a series of eight private boxes along the walls on each side.

Initially operated by the Golders Hill Picture Palace Company Ltd., it soon changed operators and was briefly re-named Louis Theatre. It was soon re-named Ionic Picture Theatre."

I saw several films in this cinema during my youth. I particularly remember watching "Fantasia" when one of its many reissues was first released in 1963. In 1975, the original building with its neo-classical façade was demolished. It was replaced by a newer building housing Sainsbury's. The planning permission for the store was conditional on building a replacement for the Ionic, which had a smaller seating capacity than the original. In September 1999, the cinema showed its last film before being closed forever.

Proceeding north along Finchley Road past the war memorial clock tower, we pass the west side of the open-air bus terminal on the south side of Golders Green Station. A detailed map surveyed in 1863 marks two buildings with two wells located on the site of the bus yard. A path led from these to the meeting of Finchley Road with North End Road. There is now a small café facing the bus yard: Bar Linda. This was opened in the early 1960s, and is still going strong. Just before reaching the railway bridge across Finchley Road, there a pub called The Refectory. It was designed by Herbert Welch (1884-1953), and was first opened as an all-electric powered restaurant in 1916. Welch also designed many other buildings in Golders Green and in the Hampstead Garden Suburb. Later, after it became a pub, it was a well-known music venue, at which musicians such as The Who, Jimi Hendrix, and Cyril Davies, have all performed.

Disused passenger walkway leading from Finchley Road into Golders Green Underground station

The Refectory pub on Finchley Road

The Bamboo Bar (see above) was under the bridge opposite a now disused covered walkway beneath a wooden canopy that used to be an entrance to the station. The interior walls of this café were lined with bamboo canes. When its owners opened the first of their chain of Spaghetti Houses (in Goodge Street), the ground floor dining room was also lined with bamboo canes. Now the premises of the former Bamboo Bar have extended into what had been its neighbour's premises (a building firm), and then enlarged to become the Artista restaurant (Italian cuisine).

Just north of the bridge on the same side of the road as Artista (and facing Rotherwick Road) is number 923 Finchley Road. During my childhood, this was the home and surgery of our family medical practitioner, Dr John Clough. His waiting room had a large fish tank. Back in the early 1960s, injections were administered using re-usable glass syringes and wide-bore re-usable needles. He 'sterilised' these in a small gas-fired water boiler that shared the gas pipe supplying the gas heater in his surgery. Dr Clough and his family were delightful, and we socialised with them. Occasionally, he and his family held parties in their back garden. This was overlooked by the brick arches supporting the tube line to Edgware. Some years later, Dr Clough shifted his surgery to a purpose-built clinic on Temple Fortune Lane. Today, number 923 has become an office building. On the same side of Finchley Road there are at least two Jewish religious institutions (including a synagogue and a yeshiva), both south of Hoop Lane.

Number 666 Finchley Road stands on the east side of the street where Middleton Road meets the main road. Between 1908, when it was founded, and a year or so ago, this was the original building of Golders Hill School ('GHS'). I attended this coeducational pre-preparatory school between about 1956, when I was 4, and 1960. When I was there, the headmistress was Miss Davies, who lived in Highgate (on Hampstead Road). She came to school on her bicycle with her two corgi dogs in a basket attached to the handlebars. They spent the day in her small office. I remember three of our teachers: Mrs Fitzgerald, who was rather large and bossy; Miss Dredge, who was slender and mild; and Miss Davis, who, unlike the rest of the staff, imparted interesting information. We learned to read and write, to recite our multiplication tables, and to do simple arithmetic. Later, we were taught some French. The brightest pupils also learnt a bit of Latin, but I was not one of this select few.

At the start of every morning, the whole school used to line up in rows in a large room on the ground floor. Our names were called out, and we had to respond by saying 'adsum', the Latin for 'I am present'. We stood facing a black and white photograph of the Matterhorn Mountain, and after the rollcall, everyone recited The Lord's Prayer at high speed. This was even though there was a significant number of Jewish pupils. I did not realise this when I was there, but often wondered why there were several days each year when many of the pupils stayed away. Later, I realised that these absentees were Jewish children celebrating religious holidays.

At lunchtime, we all ate together in groups seated at several tables. The food was not to my taste. People were encouraged eat fast. The children at the table which finished first were rewarded with pieces of Dolly Mixture (small, soft sweets in various colours). The four slowest eaters, and that included me, and a girl called Rhoda, had to sit at a special table until we had finished (or surreptitiously disposed of) what was on our plates. While we struggled with our food, everyone else was having fun outside in the playground.

Several times a week, we walked along Middleton Road towards the Hampstead Heath Extension, where we played organised games. We walked two-by-two, in a 'crocodile', along a tarmac strip between the curb stones and the paving stones. These tarred strips, we were told, were specially laid down for pupils of GHS. This was unlikely because many pavements all over Golders Green and Hampstead Garden Suburb had these black strips.

The school enlarged and moved to two mock half-timbered houses, numbers 678-680 Finchley Road. GHS was closed by its then Japanese owners in 2021.

Golders Hill School at 666 Finchley Road (in 2017)

Between Hoop Lane and the centre of Temple Fortune, Finchley Road passes several places of note. First is St Edward the Confessor Roman Catholic Church (see above). Grafton Court (number 983) stands on the site of the former Golders Green Club, about which I know nothing apart from the fact that a friend's father was a member. On the same side of Finchley Road but further north we reach number 1011 (on the corner of Portsdown Avenue), now Shiras Devorah High School, which serves the orthodox Jewish community. On its site, was located the highly praised Aida Foster Stage School, founded in 1929 by a Jewish woman Aida Foster It closed in 1970. Its graduates have included well-known names such as Barbara Windsor and Elaine Paige.

Almost opposite the former stage school, Alyth Gardens runs east from Finchley Road. The Alyth synagogue (officially known as the North Western Reform Synagogue) stands at the end of this cul-de-sac. It was built in 1936, and designed by Fritz Landauer (1883-1968), who also designed the synagogue in Augsburg (Germany), which was built 1914-17 and where members of my mother's family worshipped. His son (who modified his surname), Walter Landor (1913-1995), designed company logos, including a well-known one for Coca Cola. The congregation was founded in 1933, when it first worshipped at number 2 Meadway, a large house in Hampstead Garden Suburb. In 1936, the synagogue relocated to a parcel of land taken from the West London Synagogue's Hoop Lane cemetery. With about 3500 members, Alyth has one of the largest Jewish communities in the UK.

Continuing north along the eastern side of Finchley Road, we reach the heart of Temple Fortune's shopping centre. Two large brick buildings on the corners on each side of Hampstead Way where it joins Finchley Road contrast with the architectural mediocrity surrounding them; they are part of the Hampstead Garden Suburb. Temple Fortune House is on the north side of Hampstead Way and a similar looking building, Arcade House, is on the south side. Nikolaus Pevsner and his colleague Bridget Cherry describe these buildings in "Buildings of England. London 4: North" as follows:

"… detailed by Unwin's assistant AJ Penty (1909-1911). Their Germanic silhouettes are inspired by the mediaeval towns, like Rothenburg … Identical hipped gable ends with faintly Regency vertical iron balconies, but otherwise the buildings are subtly different: Arcade House (originally a tea room) partly timber framed, Temple Fortune House (flats) with lattice timber balconies."

Number 166 Hampstead Way, next to Temple Fortune House, is neo-Georgian style in and is the Hampstead Garden Suburb's area manager's office, Vivian House. In my childhood, much of the ground floor of Arcade House was occupied by a large store called Pullens. This shop supplied uniforms to the pupils of many north London private schools. Pullens moved away from Temple Fortune many years ago. A shop on the ground floor of Temple Fortune House was until recently the premises of Kusum Vadgama, the optometrist. Although I never made use of her services, friends gave good reports of her. I mention her because in addition to caring for people's vision, she has written some books about the history of Indian connections with the UK.

I visited Temple Fortune frequently during my childhood because when I was living in the Hampstead Garden Suburb, the nearest shops to my home were (and are still) in Temple Fortune, about half a mile's walk away. In my early teens, its main shopping attraction for me was the branch of WH Smiths, which is still in the same location as long ago. Smiths, in those far-off days, had a good stock of books and gramophone records. It was there that I bought my first classical music LP, a Music For Pleasure disc with a recording the Second Symphony by Sibelius. Buying that LP helped to begin my great love of classical music.

There was a newsagent in Temple Fortune's Bridge Lane, close to where it meets Finchley Road. It sold cultural material not then stocked by WH Smiths. This included American cartoon comics ('Superman' etc.) and Mad magazine, which I loved and on which I was prepared to spend my precious pocket money. Unlike Smiths, this shop has disappeared, but its neighbour Shutlers, a hardware shop, remains.

In my youth, Temple Fortune seemed quite a dismal area. Today (2022), the shopping centre at Temple Fortune looks better than it did when I was a child. With its cafés, some of which have outdoor tables and chairs, the district has more of a 'buzz'. Some locals have told me that nowadays it is a better (more pleasant) place to shop than Golders Green Road.

Reflecting the Jewish presence in and around Temple Fortune, it, like Golders Green Road, includes shops (e.g., Moshe's Kosher Food and Wine and Sam Stoller's) and places to eat (e.g., Platters Deli and Daniels' Bagel Bakery), which cater to the Jewish community.

Many of places that used to be part of the Temple Fortune scene during my childhood have disappeared. One of these was Brentford Nylons at the corner of Bridge Lane and a Kosher butcher (Frohwein's) a little further south along Finchley Road. At the southern end of the area, near the former Police Station, there was a shop that sold rubber hoses and cut pieces of rubber to order. This was on the corner of Finchley Road and Portsdown Mews. The former shop now houses a religious Jewish organization. Further south on Finchley Road, there was Kanu Stores, which sold everything you might need for preparing recipes from the Indian subcontinent. Joseph's bookstore, which opened after I had moved from the area, has also closed.

A narrow-fronted shop somewhere along the west side of Finchley Road housed the barber shop of Mr Lee. For many years, my friends and I used to have our haircuts there. It was quick and cheap, rather than 'haut coiffure'. Somewhere on the same side of the main road, there was Kendricks, Temple Fortune's well-stocked toy shop. To my young eyes it was a veritable treasure trove. However, once we had a poor experience there. We were just looking, minding our own business, when the owner came up to us and told us to "bugger off". As a fairly sheltered nine- or ten-year-old I was shocked. When I returned home, I related this to my parents, who were horrified that an adult could speak to children with such language. I am not sure whether I ever entered Kendricks again. The shop no longer exists. The same is true of a delicatessen called Panzers.

Temple Fortune still has the following shops that were thriving in my childhood: WHSmith, Boots the Chemist, Landy's (another chemist shop), a branch of Waitrose, and Sam Stoller's Kosher fishmonger's shop. Stoller (born 1910 in the East End) opened his store soon after WW2. Regarding this shop, I came across an odd news item in a website (www.mylondon.news) dated 22nd of June 2020:

"Metropolitan Police officers were called on Friday night (June 19) after water was seen running out of Sam Stoller & Son fishmongers, a ground floor shop on Temple Fortune Parade ... there was a "significant" water leak from the flat above ... Firefighters helped the officers force their way in only to find a sophisticated cannabis farm of more than 300 plants ... It was the hydroponic system used to water the many illegal plants that was leaking..."

Well, I had no idea that Temple Fortune could be such an exciting place. In connection with plant cultivation, there is a garden centre near to the west end of Temple Fortune Lane where it meets Finchley Road. This establishment has been there for many decades (it was in business in the early 1960s, if not before), but the off-licence shop, which used to be opposite it, is no longer there. Nearby, the Royal Oak pub that stood on the corner of Bridge Lane and Finchley Road has closed, and the building housing it has been heavily modified. It had served customers between 1861 (or earlier) and 2006.

During the 1980s, my widowed father and I often ate at an excellent Chinese restaurant, the Peking Duck, in Temple Fortune. One of the dishes I remember that we enjoyed was a starter consisting of scallops served in their shells. The restaurant closed long ago, which is a pity. The Peking Duck was close to the location of a rather uninviting looking Wimpy Bar, also now long gone.

Almost opposite WH Smiths, there is a large M&S Foodhall (opened in the 1980s). This is housed in what was during my childhood a motor car dealer's showroom. Some of its Art Deco features have been retained. North of this, stood the Odeon cinema. It stood between Birnbeck Close and Childs Way. Originally named the 'Orpheum', it was opened in October 1930. Serving both as a cinema and a theatre, it was renamed the 'Odeon' in 1945, and then later the 'Odeon Golders Green'. For a few shillings, one could spend an entire afternoon, from about two until after six pm, at the Odeon. After standing for the National Anthem, the audience watched a full-length feature film, then a documentary from the "Look at Life" series, then advertisements and film trailers, and then another full-length feature film, the latest release. Today, cinemagoers are lucky if they get anything more than the trailers and a feature film. After several lean years in the 1970s, the Odeon was demolished in May 1982 and a non-descript block of flats (Birnbeck Court) built in its place. North of this is a large block of flats with a green tiled roof and some Art Deco and Modernist features. This is The Pantiles, which was built in 1935.

North of the main line of shops, Finchley Road slopes downhill, passing a builder's supply shop housed in what used to be a petrol station, a salt beef bar, a Persian restaurant, and a long-established Japanese food centre (Atariya Foods). It then runs towards its bridge across Mutton Brook before meeting the North Circular Road at Henley's Corner (see above).

Temple Fortune House and Arcade House

UP NORTH END ROAD

North End Road leads east from the war memorial, first passing the south side of the Golders Green Station bus yard. During my childhood, the bus yard was used mainly by red London Transport and Greenline buses. Today, it is used mainly by red London Transport vehicles and long-distance National Express coaches, many of which carry passengers to and from Luton and Stansted airports.

Immediately east of the bus yard and facing North End Road, stands a large building, taller than its neighbours. It has a white stuccoed exterior, and the main entrance is on its curved, southwest corner. Designed by William Robert ('Bertie') Crewe (1860-1937), a leading British theatre architect, this building, The Hippodrome, was completed in 1913. With a seating capacity for 1500 people, it was built for the Golders Green Amusement and Development Company. It was a well-attended venue for plays and musicals both before they were shown in West End theatres as well as after they had been successful there. Every year, a lavish Christmas pantomime was staged in the Hippodrome. As a youngster, I attended several of these. I remember the theatre's interior, its auditorium with two balconies, boxes, and so on, was as grand as many of the most extravagantly decorated late 19th/early 20th century theatres in the West End. It was a West End theatre in all but its suburban location. The last 'live' performance was on the 18th of February 1968.

The Hippodrome Theatre

St Albans church

After this, the Hippodrome was taken over by the BBC. The Corporation used it as a TV studio and then later as a radio studio and concert hall. The BBC modified the auditorium and reduced its seating capacity to 700. For many years, the weekly BBC radio programme "Friday Night is Music Night", which I used to enjoy, was broadcast from it. In 2003, the BBC left the Hippodrome and put it on the market. Apparently, it was then in a tolerably good state of repair.

Sometime after 2007, the El Shaddai International Christian Centre bought the theatre. Later, it was resold, and the new owners hoped that the building could be re-purposed as an Islamic Centre, but plans for this fell through because of concerns about local traffic and parking facilities. In 2021, the Hippodrome was bought by Hillsong Church, which plans to use it for their services and to hire it out for staging events. Oddly, this has not attracted the concerns voiced against the proposed Islamic centre. An article in "The Guardian" (21st of October 2021) discussed this. Here are some interesting points from it:

"An international megachurch … has bought a renowned former theatre in north London after a campaign to prevent it from being converted into an Islamic centre … The Golders Green Hippodrome, where Marlene Dietrich, Laurence Olivier, Vera Lynn and Status Quo performed, had been owned since 2017 by Markaz El Tathgheef El Eslami (Centre for Islamic Enlightening). It paid £5.25m for the Grade II-listed building and planned to use it for conferences, seminars, youth activities, English-language classes, after-school clubs and prayers. But some residents objected, saying it would cause traffic congestion. A minority went further, suggesting that a Muslim presence in the neighbourhood could be dangerous and was undesirable ... The proposal to convert it into an Islamic centre divided the local community, which has a large Jewish presence. One objection lodged with the council claimed: 'This is going to force the Jewish population to run away, and make this beautiful neighbourhood too crowded with loads of burqas and veils.' Rabbi Mark Goldsmith, of the Golders Green Alyth Reform congregation, said such comments were 'threatening and misleading'. A letter from an interfaith forum, signed in November 2017 by representatives of Anglican, Catholic and Greek Orthodox churches, Quakers, Methodists, rabbis, imams and Sikhs, said they 'unanimously deplored and condemned the hostile and at times racist response to the new Islamic centre's opening'."

While the Hippodrome was still owned by the Muslim organisation, who had hoped to develop it, the owners, the Islamic group, generously opened the theatre for use as a covid19 vaccination centre for everyone in Golders Green, regardless of their race or religion.

Opposite the vehicle exit of the bus yard and almost facing the Hippodrome, there was a Chinese restaurant. In the 1960s, it was called the Tung Hsing. Run by a former diplomat from Chiang Kai-shek's Nationalist China and his wife, this was one of the first restaurants in London to offer genuine Pekinese-style dishes. My parents frequented it often with my sister and me. The food was tasty. On one of its walls, there were several large Chinese characters. We were told that they translated as 'all the guests feel at home'. Nearby there is still a narrow-fronted bakery, a branch of Parkway Patisserie, which used to be a branch of Lindy's bakery. This shop has served as a bakery since the 1950s, if not before.

Facing the Hippodrome across North End Road on the corner of West Heath Drive, stands Golders Green's C of E parish church: St Alban and St Michael. Designed by Giles Gilbert Scott (1880-1960), it was constructed 1932-33. Before it was built, what is now St Alban's parish hall (next to the church) was constructed in 1909 as a chapel of ease to the church of All Saints in Childs Hill. It was designed by Herbert Wills. Between 1915 and 1922, before the synagogue in Dunstan Road was ready for use, the small chapel was used not only by Christians, but also by a Jewish congregation. The latter rented it from its Anglican vicar for shabbat services and major religious festivals. It was at this parish hall that we picked up bottles of state-provided orange juice in the 1950s (see above). In the early 1960s, the future Archbishop Desmond Tutu (1931-2021) served as a curate in St Albans church.

St Albans is a simple but elegant building. Despite having some gothic features, its design is remarkably modern, although not as adventurous as Goldfinger's shop building at number 2 Golders Green Road. Many of its internal fittings were designed by Giles Gilbert Scott. The church hosts many activities including a 'South Asian Monthly Service'. The latter is offered in several languages including Urdu, Punjabi, Hindi, and English.

Annandale House

Golders Hill Terrace

Where North End Road meets West Heath Avenue, there is a large brick-built building with neo-Georgian features containing flats: Annandale House. Rated by Barnet Council as being of historic or architectural interest, I do not know when it was built. It appears on a map surveyed in 1936, and, with a differently shaped and smaller ground plan, on an 1893 map. The older map, which was surveyed long before Golders Green was anything more than a small hamlet, marks Golders Hill Terrace consisting of 10 dwellings (91 to 109 North End Road). It was then surrounded by countryside. This terrace, located between the Hippodrome and Wellgarth Road, still exists. Looking like the terraced houses along Fleet Road in Hampstead, they sit incongruously among the quite differently designed detached and semi-detached houses (built between WW1 and WW2) neighbouring them. The terrace was constructed in about 1874. During his childhood, Evelyn Waugh (1903-1966) lived in his family home, Underhill, at number 145 North End Road, which now bears a commemorative plaque. In his autobiography "A Little Learning", he noted that his mother used to visit the Terrace to carry out welfare work.

Evelyn's father Arthur bought a plot of land on North End Road in late 1906, and built the rather unattractive Underhill on it. The family began living there in September 1907. Evelyn's biographer, Selina Hastings, mentioned that in 1927, when he was living at Underhill, he wrote:
"How I detest this house and how ill I feel in it. The whole place volleys and thunders with traffic. I can't sleep well or work … The telephone bell is continually ringing, my father scampering up and down stairs, Gaspard

barking, the gardener rolling the gravel under the window and all the time the traffic. Another week of this will drive me mad."

May 1933 was the last time that Evelyn stayed at Underhill. His parents were on the point of selling it and moving to smaller accommodation in Highgate,

On Wellgarth Road, which leads off North End Road near Waugh's childhood home, there is a large building, now a block of flats. This was formerly the Wellgarth Nursery Training College. Built in 1915, it was probably designed by architect and Guild Socialist Arthur Penty (1875-1937) who worked in Parker and Unwin's architectural practice. In the 1930s, the sculptress Barbara Hepworth used the institution's childcare facilities. The staff looked after her young triplets so that she could continue working in her studio (in Hampstead) during the day. After the nursing establishment closed, it served as a youth hostel for some years before it was converted to flats.

The grounds of King Alfred School are a few yards above Waugh's home. Founded in 1898, this co-educational 'progressive' school moved from its original site in Hampstead to its present position on the former Manor House estate in 1919. It appeals to parents who wish their children to have a less conventional and less pressured educational experience than is otherwise available. Today, I believe that it is less unconventional than it used to be when I was a child. One of its buildings was designed by my late uncle, the structural engineer Sven Rindl (1921-2007).

The boundary between the Boroughs of Camden and Barnet runs across North End Road (above the school) near the main eastern entrance to Golders Hill Park. A notice marking the beginning of the Borough of Barnet stands on North End Road next to a house with some crenellations and mock Tudor features next to the park. Built by John Coore in 1786, this has long been known as 'Ivy House'. Between 1840 and 1851, it was home to CR Cockerell (1788-1863), an archaeologist, architect, and writer. In 1912, the Russian ballet dancer Anna Pavlova (1881-1931) moved into Ivy House and lived there until her death. During the 1950s, the house became part of the former (now demolished) Manor House Hospital on the corner of Hampstead Way opposite the park. Then, more recently Ivy House was home to a Jewish cultural centre. Now, it is a school: St Anthony's School for Girls.

Golders Hill Park is both in the Borough of Barnet (in which Golders Green lies) and Camden (in which Hampstead lies). The grounds of a country house, which was demolished by enemy action in 1941 during WW2, this pleasant park with its own small zoo (currently home to some ring-tailed lemurs, rheas, and wallabies amongst other creatures), tennis courts, a bandstand, ponds and streams, a stumpery, and a fine café/restaurant, is described in much more detail in my book about Hampstead, from which the following, a history of the park, is extracted:
"The park occupies the grounds of a large estate created in the 1760s by Charles Dingley (1711-1769). He made his money in the Russian sugar trade and other enterprises. He was an enthusiastic supporter of the

politician William Pitt the Elder. One of the later owners of this estate, John Coore, hired the great landscape artist Humphry Repton (1752-1815) to landscape the grounds. The penultimate owner of the estate was Queen Victoria's surgeon Sir Thomas Spencer Wells (1818-1897), inventor of the still frequently used artery forceps, now named after him. After his death, the estate with its Victorian Golders Hill Mansion was sold first to the soap magnate and historian, Thomas Barratt (1841-1914) … He sold it to a committee who wanted to save the grounds from being built over. In 1898, the grounds were opened to the public as a recreational park."

Wellgarth Road and Hampstead Way lead off North End Road and straight into Hampstead Garden Suburb, a distinctive urban development. This area, which was developed in response to the extension of the railway to Golders Green is the subject of the next part of this book.

The former Wellgarth Nursing Home

Ivy House

HAMPSTEAD GARDEN SUBURB

HISTORY

Hampstead Garden Suburb ('HGS') developed at the same time as Golders Green began to grow. However, the two neighbouring areas differ significantly. They are administered differently and are quite dissimilar in appearance. The visitor will find that in the HGS: there are no shops or places to eat and drink; there are no dividing walls or fences: only hedges; there are occasional well-manicured grassy, public open spaces; and the architecture is not only varied, but often harks back to traditional English village vernacular and historic (e.g., Georgian) styles. An important difference between Golders Green and HGS is that the development of Golders Green was in the main carried out by many private individuals, whereas HGS was developed by a single organisation, the HGS Trust, which imposed strict, immutable regulations on its design and detailed appearance. These conditions are set down in law in the Hampstead Garden Suburb Act (1906), which preceded the country's first nationwide Town Planning Act by three years. Writing in "The Story of Golders Green" (published 1979), Clive Smith and John Hall neatly summarised the difference between Golders Green and HGS:

"For Golders Green, in contrast to the highly planned and efficiently laid-out Garden Suburb, was rather a haphazard development, largely typical of what has come to be known as suburban sprawl."

HGS is an example of the activities of the innovative, utopian urban planners of the Garden City and Garden Suburb movements. They were inspired by the ideas Ebenezer Howard (1850-1928). These movements and their ideals developed during the last two decades of the 19th century. An explanation of the nature of garden suburbs can be found on the website www.gardensuburbsdirectory.co.uk:

"The concept of planned garden communities grew out of the garden villages built at the end of the 18th century by wealthy landowners for their workers and tenants.

In the late 19th and early 20th centuries Garden Suburbs were developed to provide planned estates with a similar green rural character and amenities to the earlier model villages but located near enough to cities to provide transport links to industrial and commercial centres.

The layout, architecture and landscaping were also greatly influenced by the Garden City pioneers, in particular the work of Ebenezer Howard and Parker & Unwin, although some garden city proponents disliked the concept of building suburbs and thereby enlarging the envelope of large towns."

HGS owes its existence to one woman: Dame Henrietta Barnett (née Rowland; 1851-1936). She was the wife of the cleric Canon Samuel

Barnett (1844-1913). From 1873 when they married, the couple, both social reformers, lived in the then deprived district of Whitechapel where Samuel had just become vicar of its local church, St Jude's. The area was blighted by poverty, overcrowding, and poor housing conditions. The Barnetts carried out much valuable social work in this district. One of the many things they did to bring light into the dreary, culturally deprived lives of the poor was to help found the Whitechapel Art Gallery, which opened in 1901, and is now one of London's most exciting visual art venues. This couple's worthy activities are described in detail in "Henrietta Barnett in Whitechapel" (published 2005) by my friend Micky Watkins, who does much valuable work in the HGS archives.

In 1889, the Barnetts bought Heath End House, which still stands next to the Spaniards Inn, close to the grounds of Kenwood House. They renamed their country retreat 'St Judes Cottage'. Micky Watkins noted that there was enough room in it:

"... for the Barnetts to spend their weekends, to continue training workhouse girls as domestic servants, and to accommodate convalescents from the London Hospital."

At over 400 feet above sea level, the house commanded good views over the woods and fields both to the north and the south.

All went well with the Barnett's Hampstead abode until about 1903, when plans were being made to extend the Underground into the hitherto rural district of Golders Green. The Barnetts realised that with the extension, the possibility of extensive urban development north of Hampstead became a real, and for the Barnetts also a worrying, possibility. Their concern, a selfish one, was that their views over the countryside north of their home would be submerged under a sea of bricks and mortar.

As Jonquil Griffiths described in her book "Henrietta Barnett and he First Class High School" (published 2013), Henrietta and Samuel became involved with the activities of The Hampstead Heath Protection Fund. I had been founded in 1866 by a banker, J Gurney Hoare, a member of the Hoare banking family who had a house (the 18th century Heath House) near Hampstead Heath and Jack Straws Castle. In 1884, this group of activists prevented Parliament Hill Fields from being built on, and in 1897 saved the grounds of the Golders Hill estate from a similar fate, and in the process creating Golders Hill Park.

When, in about 1903, the Barnetts learned that the Trustees of the Eton College Estate were planning to sell their land north of Spaniards Road to housing developers, they joined the Protection Fund (or Society) in their attempts to preserve it from becoming covered with houses. Springing into action, they helped form a committee, 'The Heath Extension Council', to buy over 320 acres of land (mainly fields and woodland) north of their home, that over which they could see, to extend Hampstead Heath, and thus prevent it from being built on. This land, which is now the Hampstead Heath Extension, was costly. The Extension was partly paid for by the London County Council, who opened it to the public as a park for public use (it is now maintained by the Corporation of London). However, the land purchase required much more money. Henrietta realised that by buying some more land and developing it for housing, this would help to pay for the land (the view from St Jude's Cottage) that she wanted to save from urban development. In a book about an earlier garden suburb, Brentham in Ealing (founded 1901), its author Aileen Reid noted: "… to save the Heath from development … by 1903 Barnett was negotiating to buy a further 243 acres to build a 'garden suburb' that would be both architecturally varied and socially diverse."

Henrietta was familiar with the works of urban planning reformers such as Ebenezer Howard and the architects Raymond Unwin (1863-1940) and Richard Parker (1867-1947). The two architects had already been involved in both garden city (e.g., Letchworth Garden City) and garden suburb planning (e.g., New Earswick near York). It was to these two men that Henrietta turned to plan the construction of her garden suburb in which she hoped that people from all social classes could live together in a pleasant environment, the antithesis of what existed in the slums of Whitechapel. Later, Raymond Unwin wrote in his "Town planning in practice; an introduction to the art of designing cities and suburbs" (published in 1909) that Henrietta:

"… has referred to the many evils which result from large areas being inhabited entirely by people of one limited class. Indeed, it was one of her special aims in promoting the Hampstead Garden Suburb Trust to show to how much greater extent the intermingling of the different classes might be brought about. It is not within the power of the town planner to alter the prejudices of people, or to prevent entirely the growing up of the East

End and West End in a town; but a good deal may be done in this direction by care and forethought; certainly within limits, more or less wide, there is no difficulty in mingling houses of different sizes."

Rather than becoming a mingling of social classes as Henrietta was hoping, today the only real mingling in HGS is of differently sized houses.

In 1906, Henrietta and others set up the first HGS Trust, which owned the freehold of the land and oversaw the development of the new garden suburb. One of its founding members was Henry Vivian (1868-1930), who founded the earlier Brentham Garden Suburb. Henrietta's idea was (as quoted from www.hgstrust.org/the-suburb/history/index.shtml) that:

"The houses will not be put in uniform lines nor in close relationship built regardless of each other, or without consideration for picturesque appearance. Great care will be taken that the houses shall not spoil each other's outlook, while the avoidance of uniformity or of an institutional aspect will be obtained by the variety of the dwellings, always provided that the fundamental principle is complied with that the part should not spoil the whole, nor that individual rights be assumed to carry the power of working communal wrong."

According to the same source, Henrietta considered that:

"… the model for the Suburb was the country town, but the emphasis was on the country rather than the town. She wanted to show 'how thousands of people, of all classes of society, of all sorts of opinions, and all standards of income, can live in helpful neighbourliness', and that this was to be achieved in such a way that 'from every part there shall be good views or glimpses of distant country'"

HGS is built on hilly terrain. Throughout, the housing density is lower than in most other London suburbs. As for mixing of the social classes, this did not happen. The lower cost, smaller houses were clustered together in the so-called 'Artisans Quarter', which was first to be constructed (in 1907) on lower lying land. The first two homes that were built are numbers 140 and 142 Hampstead Way. Larger homes for the better-off (middle and upper middle classes) were built higher up on the slopes of the hills upon which Central Square and other parts of the Suburb are located. Even at the outset, when participants joined the HGS Trust Ltd, there was a financial barrier to be crossed: the initial investment was £5. This was beyond the means of the truly needy; only skilled artisans, clerks, and tradesmen could afford it. Thus, from the start, HGS excluded the kind of people that the Barnetts assisted in the East End. And, looking ahead, today it is only the wealthy who can afford to buy properties in HGS. Nevertheless, the construction of the HGS saved what is now Hampstead Heath Extension from being buried under suburban housing.

Part of the Great Wall running alongside Hampstead Heath Extension

I mentioned above that there are no walls or fences dividing properties in the HGS. There is, however, a long stretch of wall that separates part of the of the Suburb from the Extension. Built to resemble a mediaeval town wall, this, the Great Wall with its small lookouts, was designed by the Afro-Caribbean architect Charles Wade (1883-1956), working for Parker and Unwin. The outbreak of WW1 put an end to its completion. It is half as long as was planned.

LUTYENS AND CENTRAL SQUARE

Designed to be the throbbing communal heart of HGS, Central Square is a failure. Pevsner and Cherry noted in their "Buildings of England: London 4: North":

"Unwin's first plans had included shops along the approaches, but as built by Sir Edwin Lutyens, appointed consultant architect in 1906, the shops were omitted and the square became a high-minded enclave of churches and public buildings with a fringe of smart houses."

The writers pointed out that without shops, the square never became a true social centre. In fact, most of the time it is an almost deserted open space. Lutyens (1869-1944) did not get on well with Henrietta Barnett. In her book "The architect and his wife: a life of Edwin Lutyens" (published in 2002), Jane Ridley wrote:

"Lutyens was no progressive. He had no interest in using architecture to change the way people lived, to eliminate servants or smooth social divisions … He disliked the bossiness of social reformers such as Mrs Barnett. Ugly, squalid towns such as Manchester depressed him, but he didn't see town planning as a motor for change. All he wanted was to build beautiful buildings: 'Loveliness alone is akin to godliness and whilst ugliness is countenanced and excused Hell is possible.'"

Later in her book Ridley recorded that Lutyen's wife Emily had written to him after he had fled abroad in 1908 (having had disagreements with Henrietta):

"'I am glad you went,' she wrote, 'as you needed rest and change, only you must work up the Hampstead affair and not let grass grow under your feet, or Mrs Barnett will put you in the wrong again.'"

Despite his differences with Mrs Barnett, Lutyens left his architectural mark on the square. These are his buildings built before he drew up plans for most of his buildings in British India, notably in New Delhi. As Mary Lutyens described in her book "Edwin Lutyens" (published in 1991), his work in the suburb was of importance for his future career:

"At the beginning of 1912 Lord Crewe, Secretary of State for India, approached Reginald Blomfield, President of the Royal Institute of British Architects, to recommend an architect to serve on a commission of three experts to advise the Government of India on the siting and laying out of the new capital. Blomfield recommended Lutyens on the strength of his country houses …his work in Johannesburg … and for Hampstead Garden Suburb. Sir Richmond Ritchie, Permanent Secretary for India, then sent for Lutyens and asked him if he would be willing to serve on the Commission..."

Incidentally, in connection with the above, Lutyens was already married to the daughter of a Viceroy of India.

The Free Church with its dome stands on the north side of the square. It was begun in 1911 and only completed in the 1960s. Facing it on the south side is St Jude's Church, which was built mainly between 1909 and 1911. Its design was one of the causes of disagreement between Barnett and Lutyens. Pevsner and Cherry considered it to be one of Lutyens's most successful buildings. It has a tall spire, which can be seen from miles around. With its tunnel (or barrel) vaulting over the nave, its ceiling paintings by Walter Starmer (1877-1961) painted 1919-1930, and extensive use of internal brickwork, I have always felt that it is a quite unusual church. Used for regular religious services, it also hosts classical music concerts, and has been used for recording music CDs.

Lovers of the Harry Potter films should note that St Jude's church stars in one of them as has been noted in a pamphlet, "Barnet Healthy Heritage Walks", issued by the Borough Barnet. Discussing Heathgate, which runs downhill from St Jude's to the Heath Extension, it remarked:

"You may be interested to know that you are now walking in the footsteps of young wizard Harry Potter on his way to his muggle born friend Hermione Grainger's parents' house, as seen with St Jude's in the background in the 2010 film 'Harry Potter and the Deathly Hallows: Part 1'"

The Free Church on Central Square

The Institute on Central Square

Top: St Judes
Bottom: Friends Meeting House

On the east side of the vast square, stands The Institute, which was designed by Lutyens with later additions by JCS Soutar (1881-1951), who carried out much other work in HGS. Built from 1908 onwards, it was intended to be used both as a cultural centre and part of the Henrietta Barnett School (founded 1911). Pevsner and Cherry dismiss it as "Feeble Neo-Georgian". The school was founded by Henrietta Barnett, who was an early pioneer of female education. One wall of the Institute bears a commemorative inscription:

"This stone was unveiled by Her Royal Highness The Princess Margaret on 2nd of July 1957 to commemorate the jubilee of the Hampstead Garden Suburb 1907 1957."

I was only five years old that day, but I remember it well. I was visiting my aunt and her children, who lived in Raeburn Close, which leads off Wildwood Road, where I stood with a Union Jack flag in my hand. As Princess Margaret drove past us, I waved the flag: my brief brush with royalty!

Across the square near the tennis courts on its western side, there is a simple small stone memorial to Henrietta Barnett beneath four bronze arches. This was designed by Lutyens in about 1938.

Monument to Dame Henrietta Barnett by Lutyens
(on Central Square)

Soutar took over the direction and planning of the development of HGS from Unwin in 1918. The parts of the Suburb built after Soutar took the helm differ from that which was constructed before. This was largely because, as a website text (www.hgs.org.uk/history) explained, it was:

"… far more to the decision by the Old Hampstead Garden Suburb Trust and the co-partnership companies to relinquish the most important social and physical ideals which had guided the Garden Suburb's planners before the War, largely as a result of the inflation of building costs in 1919-20. Apart from the completion of areas laid out earlier, the development of the Garden Suburb after 1918 consisted almost entirely of conventional houses for sale. There was no attempt to create a socially balanced community, even though that had been achieved to a remarkable extent in the earlier part. This renunciation of social idealism was paralleled by a surrender of the architectural and landscaping values."

North Square and South Square lie on either side of Central Square. These green spaces are surrounded by blocks of flats and 'smart' houses. Some of the houses in North Square and Erskine Hill leading north from it were also designed by Lutyens. Overall, what Lutyens created in the Suburb is, although elegant, not to my taste. Number 1 South Square was the home of the founder of HGS, Henrietta Barnett, between 1915 and her death in 1936. She moved into this house two years after her husband died.

At the east side of North Square, there is an attractive low building set in a lovely garden: The Friends Meeting House. It was designed by Fred

Rowntree (1860-1927) and built in 1913. Its shape was based on the design of the 1688 Jordans Meeting House in Buckinghamshire. Next door to this on the western end of Northway, stands the Free Church Hall, also known as the Tea House. Built in 1923 by the HGS Trust as a sports pavilion and changing rooms, it has served other purposes, mainly for the local community's benefit, since then.

Central Square is usually used as an open space to walk, sit, or play tennis. During my childhood, I used to cycle along its paths and play ballgames with my friends, who lived nearby on Erskine Hill (in neighbouring houses designed by Lutyens). Occasionally, the Square temporarily achieves its founders' original purpose when fetes are held on its lawns.

BIG AND LITTLE WOODS

The planners of HGS preserved a couple of patches of woodland, which are remnants of an extensive forest that existed over 1000 years ago. They were probably part of a tract of land given to Waldhere (died between 705 and 716), a Bishop of London, in 704. The woodland remained property of the Church until 1911, when it was leased to the HGS Trust. In 1933, the freehold of this land was transferred to Finchley Urban District Council, and in 1965 it was taken over by its successor the London Borough of Barnet. Big Wood covers 18 acres, and Little Wood covers 3 acres.

At the Temple Fortune Hill entrance to Big Wood, there is a wooden gate that commemorates 29 residents of HGS, who died during WW2. It stands on what was once an 8th century boundary. The wood can also be accessed from Northway, Denman Drive South, and from near Northway Gardens (which run alongside Mutton Brook). Big Wood, which slopes gently downwards towards Mutton Brook, has many streams and such a dense growth of trees (mainly oak, hornbeams, and wild cherry) that one feels as if one is deep within a huge forest. It is only at the very edges of the wood that one can catch glimpses of the houses surrounding it.

There is a report that circus elephants used to be kept in a field that existed between Big and Little Woods before the construction of houses in this location (now Denman Drive North and South). Colin Gregory wrote (www.hgs.org.uk):

"Before leaving this story, we should pay our respects to one of the last occupiers of Park Farm: the circus proprietor Lord' George Sanger ... His descendants continued the circus in operation until the 1960s. It is said that when he owned Park Farm he allowed the circus animals to winter on his land. An elderly resident of Denman Drive – constructed in 1908 on what was once Westminster Abbey's land – used to recall 'elephants grazing' in the field between Big Wood and Little Wood, before Denman Drive North and Denman Drive South – constructed in 1912 on what was once the Bishop's land – were completed."

Little Wood, whose history is the same as that of Big Wood, contains one of London's lesser-known performance spaces: a small open-air theatre. This was created in 1920 by the Play and Pageant Union, one of two drama groups that later merged to form the Garden Suburb Theatre. It was restored in 1997, and now looks like it would benefit from some more work. The stage is a flat clearing in the woods, surrounded by trees and bushes. The audience sits on a stepped auditorium consisting of three layers of paving stones set in a curve around the stage.

The theatre in Little Wood occupies an important place amongst my childhood memories. It was here when I was about ten years old, back in the early 1960s, that I first saw a performance of Shakespeare's "A Midsummer Night's Dream". It must have been on a summer evening when I watched this with a sense of wonder that still lives with me. Apart from a few logs, there were no other props. The actors and actresses appeared on, and disappeared from, the simple stage almost magically, popping through gaps between the trees and bushes surrounding the theatre.

I do not know what The Bard was thinking when he created "The Dream", but I feel that he would have approved of its being acted out in on the sylvan stage in Little Wood. Furthermore, I think that he would have appreciated a play, which contains six amateur actors in its plot, being performed by a troupe of amateur actors such as we were watching that evening long ago. Since watching that play in Little Wood so many years ago, I have seen several other performances of "A Midsummer Night's Dream", and only one has given me as much pleasure as that. It was a recent (2019) staging of the play directed by Nicholas Hytner at the relatively new Bridge Theatre near London's Tower Bridge. A review of this noted:

"The theatre becomes the forest – a dream world of flying fairies, contagious fogs and moonlight revels."

And the result at the Bridge was wonderful, although seeing the play in a real forest (Little Wood, in my case) is hard to beat.

Returning to the little theatre in Little Wood one day in 2020 when it was out of use because of the covid19 pandemic, it kindled many happy memories. Although I had not visited that theatre for many decades, it looked just as I remembered it.

HGS MODERNE, MARKET PLACE, AND WW2

Although HGS began to be built in the early 20th century and continued into the late 1930s, remarkably few of its buildings reflect the exciting and revolutionary developments in architecture that were flourishing elsewhere during the '20s and '30s. Even in the late 1930s many buildings were designed, as were those in the early days of HGS, in architectural styles that looked back nostalgically at traditional English village architecture and historical building styles. However, many of the earlier buildings have features influenced by the Arts and Craft Movement, which was in fashion in the early years of the 20th century. There are a few exceptions to the evocation of the past exhibited in most of the buildings designed by the Suburb's architects. These include some houses built in the 'moderne' form of the Art Deco style, which had its heyday between the two World Wars.

Lytton Close

A few Art Deco houses can be found in Kingsley Close near the Market Place and Mutton Brook. They were designed by the architects Herbert Welch (1884–1953), Nugent Francis Cachemaille-Day (1896–1976), and Felix Lander (1890-1960). There is a larger number of them in the area through which the following roads run: Neville Drive, Spencer Drive, Carlyle Close, Holne Chase, Rowan Walk, and Lytton Close. The part of HGS in which these roads run was developed from about 1927 onwards, mainly between 1935 and 1938. So, it is unsurprising that examples of what was then fashionable in architecture can be found in this part of the suburb. According to an informative document (www.hgstrust.org/documents/area-13-holne-chase-norrice-lea.pdf) about this part of HGS:

"… A relatively restricted group of established architects undertook much development such as M. De Metz, G. B. Drury and F. Reekie, Welch, Cachemaille-Day and Lander, and J. Oliphant. H. Meckhonik was a developer/builder and architects in his office may have designed houses attributed to him."

Meckhonic was also involved in the construction of the Art Deco Belvedere Court (see above). Most of the Art Deco houses on Spencer Drive and Carlyle Close leading off from it are unexceptional buildings, whose principal Art Deco features are the metal framed windows (made by the Crittall company) with some curved panes of glass. Fitted with any other design of windows, these houses would lose their Art Deco appearances. Number 1, Neville Drive displays more features of the style than the houses in Spencer Drive and Carlyle Close. There is, however, one house on Spencer Drive that is unmistakably 'moderne': it is number

28 built in 1934 without reference to tradition. It is an adventurous design compared with the other buildings in the street.

Numbers 13 and 24 Rowan Walk, a pair of almost identical buildings which stand on either side of the northern end of the street where it meets Linden Lea, stand out from the crowd. They have flat roofs and 'moderne' style Crittall Windows. Built in the 1930s, they are cubic in form: unusual rather than elegant.

I have saved the best for last: Lytton Close. This cul-de-sac is lined by a wonderful ensemble of Art Deco houses. They have: balconies that resemble the deck railings of oceanic liners; flat roofs that serve as sun decks; curved Crittall windows; and glazed towers housing staircases. Built in 1935, they were designed by CG Winburne. Although I lived for almost three decades in HGS, and used to walk around it a great deal, I missed seeing Lytton Close until August 2022. It is one of London's finer examples of modern domestic architecture constructed between the two world wars. Although most of the Art Deco buildings in HGS are not as spectacular as edifices made in this style in Lytton Close and further afield in, say, Bombay, the employment of this distinctive style injected a little modernity in an area populated with 20th century buildings that mostly attempted to create a village atmosphere typical of earlier times. The architects, who adopted backward-looking styles, did this to create the illusion that dwellers in the HGS would not be living on the doorstep of a big city but, instead, far away in a rural arcadia.

Many of the Art Deco Houses are close to Market Place, a shopping centre strung along both sides of Lyttelton Road and its continuation Falloden Way. This shopping centre was part of Unwin's design and consists of unremarkable 1930s buildings with ground floor shops and flats above them. There used to be a children's shoe shop in Market Place, when I was a young child. My mother bought shoes for me there, but did not allow the staff to use their special x-ray machine (for checking the fit of shoes) on me. My mother either knew of, or was concerned about, the damage that x-radiation can cause to children's growing bones. Between Market Place and East Finchley station, there is more of HGS, but most of this was built in the late 1920s and early '30s, and is less attractive than the older parts of the Suburb.

There are several newer (post-1930s) buildings dotted around HGS, but they are few and rarely of architectural excellence. One of them, which interested me, is number 67 Hampstead Way. It stands facing the Heath at the Hampstead Way end of Wild Hatch, was not built at the same time as its pre-WW1 neighbours. From its design, I would guess that number 67 was put up in the 1960s. It is located above a stream that flows under it from the Heath Extension. I recall that in the 1960s, it and the nearby field on the Heath were subject to flooding when the stream was in spate.

It is worth wandering along Wild Hatch (a track that existed during the 18th century and before) to the place where the footpath becomes a road. There, you will see a building with large garage doors surmounted by a gable containing many dovecote apertures. This is believed to have been the 'motor house' for number 85 Hampstead Way (built before WW1, as were most of the houses in that road).

On the Heath Extension close to number 67 but now hidden by a dense, impenetrable growth of bushes, there is (or was) a raised platform made of flat concrete slabs. This was both visible and accessible during my childhood. It served as a base for anti-aircraft guns during WW2.

Between the 7th of October 1940 and the 6th of June 1941, many high explosive bombs were dropped on Golders Green. Several fell on HGS. According to a map on bombsite.org, at least one of them landed on Hampstead Way close to where the current post-war number 67 stands today. However, I do not know for sure whether bomb damage was the reason that this post-war house was built on the site of a bombed building. Other structures in HGS, which were badly damaged by bombing during WW2 included the Hampstead Golf Club, the Suburb's Club House on Willifield Way, and its neighbour the school on Childs Way. Near the school, there were trench shelters that protected many people from being injured. However, in the heavy raid on that part of the Suburb, 12 people were killed and many more injured.

Smith and Hall recorded in their book that during WW2, 242 people were killed in the Borough of Hendon (in which both Golders Green and HGS were located), 500 were seriously injured, and 20,000 properties were damaged. The clubhouse was rebuilt as Fellowship House. Its first sod was dug by Princess Margaret when she visited HGS in 1957.

Houses designed by Lutyens on Erskine Hill

Meadway Court

The Orchard

The first two houses built in Hampstead Garden Suburb

A STROLL THROUGH THE SUBURB

I have outlined some of the things that make HGS a place of special interest. Using a good map, you can now join me on a walk around it and explore the variety of architectural styles on display there. Commencing at Golders Green station, walk north along Finchley Road, and then turn right into Hoop Lane. On your way, you will pass Rotherwick Road, which is entirely in the HGS, and further along, Middleton Road, which is not. Parallel to the latter and closer to Hoop Lane, the western stretch of Corringham Road is outside the HGS, but its continuation eastwards beyond its junction with Rotherwick Road is within the Suburb.

Hoop Lane stretches gently uphill, passing between the crematorium on its south side and the Jewish cemeteries on its northern side. Cross a small triangular garden surrounded by roads (it had no name during my childhood, but is now called Meadway Gate Open Space) to reach the western end of Meadway. Number 2 Meadway always fascinates me with its tall bay window that extends from ground level to just below the eaves. Built in 1911-12, it was designed by Edwin and James Palser. Where Meadway crosses Hampstead Way, there is a distinctive terrace of houses (built 1908-09), which curves around the southeast corner and has some Arts and Crafts features. As a child, I thought it unattractive, and my opinion has changed little since then. However, others consider it to be one of the great works by the architect Mackay Hugh Baillie-Scott (1865-

1945). It is an architectural ensemble in keeping with the generally backward-looking (or historically inspired) designs employed by the Suburb's architects.

Turn left into Hampstead Way. On the corner of this road and Hill Close, you will see number 36, the detached house where I was brought up. Closes, often with footpaths at their ends, and occasional grassy open spaces, such as the one at the bifurcation of Hampstead Way and Willifield Way, are typical features of the Suburb. Walk north along Willifield Way. The composer Eric Coates (1886-1957) lived at number 7 between 1925 and 1931, and the engineer Ove Arup (1895-1988) lived at number 28 between 1932 and 1939. These men were two of a great number of noteworthy people, who have lived in the suburb. After passing what resembles a small village green, Willifield Road crosses Temple Fortune Hill before flanking a grassy open space beyond which there is a housing complex called The Orchard. This was originally built (in 1909) as flats for the elderly. Some newer (post-WW2) buildings have been added to the ensemble.

Walk along the footpath that goes through The Orchard to reach Hampstead Way again, and then turn right. The road passes Asmuns Hill and heads west towards Temple Fortune. On this stretch, numbers 140 and 142 Hampstead Way are the first two houses to have been constructed in the HGS (in 1907). The bases of these houses are inscribed with sets of initials. I guess that these were the initials of people involved in the founding of HGS. Hampstead Way is one of the longest roads in HGS. The sinuous nature of its southern half reflects the fact that it was originally laid out to follow old field boundaries.

Turn around, and head up the slope of Asmuns Hill to reach another grassy space flanked by Willifield Way. This, Willifield Green, is yet another attempt to create a village-like atmosphere in the Suburb. On the east side of this, stands Fellowship House, which was built after WW2 to replace the Club House that stood on this site, but was badly damaged during WW2. A footpath leads west from the green towards Childs Way. It passes the grounds of the Garden Suburb Junior School, which was opened in 1913. Part of the original building was rebuilt in 1960 to replace what had been destroyed in WW2.

Return along Willifield Way to Asmuns Hill and continue uphill to Erskine Hill. Turn right and at the end of this thoroughfare, having first crossed Temple Fortune Hill, you will see the dome and north side of The Free Church on Central Square. If you continue east along Temple Fortune Hill, you reach an entrance to Big Wood. At the top of Erskine Hill, turn left onto a road called North Square and soon you will pass the Quaker Meeting House. Next to it at the top end of Northway, you will see the Tea House (HGS Free church Hall).

Garden Suburb Junior School

From the Tea House, it is only a few yards' walk to Central Square. The attractions of this open space have been described in a previous section. Head away from the Square along Southway. Harold Wilson, former Prime Minister, lived at both numbers 10 and 12 (until 1964). Return to Central Square and into South Square, lined on its southwest side by a block of flats. Henrietta Barnett lived the last years of her life in a house (number 1) on the west side of South Square. Heathgate, overlooked by the spire of St Jude's, leads downhill from South Square towards the Heath Extension. A footpath leads from the end of Heathgate to an open space, Sunshine Corner, surrounded on three sides by brick walls and overlooking the fields of the Extension towards the slopes of Hampstead. The walls form part of the Suburb's so-called Great Wall (see above).

Follow the cinder footpath east along the north edge of the Heath Extension until after 333 yards, you reach a narrow path that leads north and opens into Meadway Close. The economist Sir Lionel Robbins (1898-1984), one of my father's senior colleagues at the London School of Economics, lived on the west side of the Close. Turn right onto Meadway and soon you will pass what looks a bit like a Cambridge college quadrangle: a block of flats called Meadway Court. Erected in 1913, this residential complex was designed by George Lister Sutcliffe (1864-1915), who designed many other buildings in both HGS and in Brentham Garden Suburb. He succeeded Raymond Unwin as consultant architect for HGS. Turn right into Wildwood Road. Number 8 was the birthplace of the actress Elizabeth Taylor (1932-2011). The designer Frank Pick

(1871-1941), who worked for London Transport, lived at number 15, a grand house. For much of its length, Wildwood Road skirts the Heath Extension. As the road ascends gently towards the ridge separating HGS from Hampstead, the houses along it tend to be larger and grander than others in the Suburb. The pianist Dame Myra Hess (1890-1965) lived at number 48. Ingram Avenue, lined with large houses, homes of very well-off folk, leads to Winnington Road, also lined with homes of the wealthy, leads to Hampstead Lane and Kenwood. Continue along Wildwood Road. At the end of Turner Close, which leads from Wildwood Road to the tiny Turners Wood (a remnant of an ancient wood), there is a large house in which the philosopher, a refugee from Communist Hungary, Imre Lakatos (1922-1974) lived until his death.

The Hampstead Golf Club and its course lie enclosed between Wildwood Road, Ingram Avenue, Winnington Road, and Neville Drive. This nine-hole course, created on land that had been owned by the Bishops of London, was ready for use in 1893. Its members have included notable persons such as Alastair Sim, Lord Soper, Tim Brooke-Taylor, and former Prime Minister Harold Wilson. It was while Wilson was a member that a former Mayor of Finchley, Mr Frank Davis, alleged that there was a prejudice against Jews applying for membership. According to an article in the January 1965 issue of "AJR Information", Mr Davis wrote to the Prime Minister asking him to leave the club because of its supposed bias against Jewish people. Wilson replied:

"... five of my last six rounds in the club have been with a Jewish partner. I was in fact put-up for the club by a well-known Jewish member."

Mr Davis responded by saying that although there was no bar against Jewish or coloured people, several Jewish people had complained that it was made more difficult for them to join. In his book on anti-Semitism, Anthony Julius noted that Jewish people were excluded from nearby Finchley Golf Club in the early 1960s. The "Jewish Chronicle" (22nd of June 2017) recorded that in the late 1950s:

"...a number of Jews — including Shirley Porter, then a young Liberal activist — had applied to join the Finchley golf club. Each had had their membership refused; not an uncommon occurrence at golf clubs at this time."

I remember an old Jewish friend, who lived in the Suburb, telling me that he had to join the distant Roehampton Club to play golf because the clubs near to his home turned away Jewish applicants. As the years have passed, things have changed for the better as far as joining golf clubs is concerned. The Hampstead Golf Club's membership application form now includes the words:

"Hampstead Golf Club (HGC) prides itself on being a friendly and inclusive club ..."

Top: Raeburn Close
Bottom: former home of Frank Pick

Wildwood Road bends and runs west until it meets the southern stretch of Hampstead Way. This stretch of Wildwood separates the 'old' wooded Hampstead Heath from the fields of the more open Heath Extension, which Henrietta Barnett helped to preserve. Wyldes Farm, which overlooks the western end of Wildwood Road and the sharp bend made by Hampstead Way is in the old part of the Heath and is part of Hampstead's North End hamlet (discussed in detail in my book about Hampstead). It was here that Raymond Unwin, the planner of HGS, lived and worked from about 1905 to his death. The old farmhouse was purchased by Henrietta Barnett and others. Much of the Suburb's planning was carried out within it and its neighbouring barn, both still standing.

Follow along Wildwood Road, heading west, and then you will reach the stretch of Hampstead Way running to North End Road. Turn left on to the latter, and you can enjoy a pint at the historic Old Bull and Bush pub. Turn right, and you will pass an entrance to Golders Hill Park close to its café. Head downhill and you will soon reach Golders Green station. By following the walk described above, you will have had a reasonable sample of the 'flavour' of HGS.

Had you entered Big Wood at the end of Temple Fortune Lane, you could have followed paths through the trees to reach the Market Place and Mutton Brook, already described above. If, on the other hand you had left Wildwood Road by walking along Kingsley Way, you would have reached the part of the Suburb containing many Art Deco Houses (see above). If you are not feeling too energetic, you can walk along Rotherwick Road and then turn right into Corringham Road, which leads to Hampstead Way on the east side of the Heath Extension. By walking northeast across the grass, you will reach the Great Wall, and then you can follow the latter half of the walk as described above. The possibilities are limited only by how enthusiastic you are about walking.

If, however, you do not enjoy exploring by foot, there is an easy alternative. This is the H2 bus, which follows a circular route through much of HGS. It passes all the places mentioned above and a few more. It provides a speedy way to see most of the Suburb. Using the GPS service on your mobile 'phone, you can keep track of where the bus takes you as you speed past the sights mentioned in my text. Incidentally, you can ask the driver to drop you off almost anywhere on the route.

As you strolled (or drove) around HGS, you might have wondered about the names of its roads and closes. Clive Smith and John Hall quoted Henrietta Barnett as saying:
"… we decided that the East End of the Suburb should bear the names of great lawyers such as Erskine, Denman, and Chatham; the North end those of poets – Wordsworth, Coleridge, and the South end those of English artists – Turner, Linnell, Reynolds, Morland, Cotman, Raeburn, Constable and so on."
Smith and Hall also mentioned that some of the founders of the Suburb have their names recorded in street names (e.g., Vivian, Falloden,

Lyttleton, and Lytton), but others, including the architects Unwin, Parker, and Lutyens, have not been assigned as names of thoroughfares.

Most of the roads in the Suburb were laid down after its creation. These include the two main arteries: Meadway and Hampstead Way. The latter was (and might still be) used as a 'rat run' by drivers wishing to avoid the traffic in Temple Fortune and Golders Green.

Two roads pre-date the Suburb. They were already in existence long ago: they are marked on maps prepared in the 1860s, but were likely to have been present long before that time. Hoop Lane is one of them. The other is Temple Fortune Lane and its southern extension, Wild Hatch which is a cul-de-sac with a footpath leading from its end to Hampstead Way. On old (pre-HGS) maps, Wild Hatch had a few cottages along it and then followed the same course as it does now, but ended in the fields that were later to become the Heath Extension.

A HGS CHILDHOOD

I could write much more about the history and architecture of HGS, but this has been done before (and in detail) in other books, notably that by Pevsner and Cherry and in a series of reports available online (www.hgstrust.org/the-suburb/character-appraisal.shtml). So, instead I will describe what I remember of being a child in the HGS in the 1950s and 1960s.

Top: The author's childhood home on Hampstead Way) (1908)
Bottom: A grand house on Wildwood Road (1928)

My parents bought our family home, number 36 Hampstead Way (on the corner of Hill Close), in about 1950. It was a house designed for reasonably well-off middle-class families. On higher ground than, and facing, a row of smaller houses designed for artisans and their families, it is a good example of what Henrietta Barnett was optimistically trying to achieve: namely, the mixing of different social classes. Still standing, number 36 is a substantial detached building with a garden, a backyard, and a separate garage. When we lived there, the rooms on the ground floor were as follows: my father's study (originally the formal dining room); a sitting room that looked out over the garden; a breakfast room and neighbouring kitchen. Upstairs, there were four bedrooms, a bathroom, and a separate toilet. There were also other small rooms and a space beneath the staircase. They were used for storage or drying laundry. The backyard, which was outside the kitchen and behind the garage (which was separate from the house), also provided access to a toilet, which could not be reached without leaving the house. When my parents acquired the house, it had the name 'Inverugie' painted above the front porch. Not liking this name, my parents had it painted over with whitewash. If you look at the front porch carefully today, you will still be able to discern the slightly raised letters of the name beneath the paint.

When they moved into number 36, my parents were amongst the youngest couples in the neighbourhood. Consequently, when I was born in 1952, there were scarcely any other children of my age living nearby. Our neighbours on Hill Close were an elderly, friendly couple, Mr and Mrs

Palmer. Next door to us on Hampstead Way, there was a single lady, Miss Reinecke, who was older than my parents, and although she greeted us in the street, we never knew much about her. Another ageing couple, the Caldwells, lived opposite us, and later moved to number 32, which faced number 36 on the other corner of Hill Close (there is no number 34). If they had children, they were older than me. The Arnotts on Hill Close had a couple of children: one older and one younger than me. So, as far as having neighbourhood 'kids' of my age to play with, there were none for me. The nearest children with whom I played in the HGS were my cousins in Raeburn Close, and a school friend who lived in Temple Fortune Lane. Both places were about 10 minutes' brisk walk from our house. By the time I was ten, I met three boys, who became lifelong friends: they lived in neighbouring semi-detached houses designed by Lutyens on Erskine Hill, north of North Square. Before that, I had made friends with Micaela ('Mica') Comberti (1952-2003), whom I met at a tender age when we both attended Miss Schreuer's kindergarten in Hoop Lane. Her family lived in HGS, but further south than us. With a German mother and Italian father, with whom my parents became friendly, Mica became a noted concert violinist. Her brother, Sebastian, is a professional 'cellist.

By the time my sister was born (after 1955), there were more young children in our immediate vicinity. My sister was friendly with one of the daughters of the Arnott family, who lived near us on Hill Close. I was also friendly with the younger daughter of the Pinguet family, who lived opposite us on Hampstead Way (after the Caldwells had shifted). Around the time when my sister was born, the Terry family, who also lived opposite us, had given birth to the first of their two sons, whom I considered too young to be my playmates. Nowadays, there is no shortage of young children in HGS.

HGS was an extremely quiet place during my childhood. There was far less motor traffic than nowadays and no bus service. The nearest bus stops were on Finchley Road and in the Market Place. Even though we lived only a few feet below St Jude's Church, we heard no church bells: ringing of such bells was forbidden by the founders of HGS. Some days, one could hear trains moving at Golders Green Station and in its neighbouring sidings, which were about 770 yards away (as the crow flies). On a few weekend afternoons, usually in summer, occasional strands of music could be heard coming over the air from the bandstand at Golders Hill Park (which I have never seen in use). Otherwise, the Suburb was almost deathly quiet.

I have already mentioned that there were no shops in HGS (apart from in the Market Place). There were two exceptions to this. One was a small electrical supply shop on Hampstead Way, a few yards away from Arcade House on Finchley Road in Temple Fortune. It was housed in a single-storey outhouse of Arcade House and is currently (2022) the premises of MJO Arts. The other place was Mendel's garage and petrol station, which used to be in a square surrounded by blocks of flats at the end of Corringway (a cul-de-sac leading off Corringham Road). This place, where my parents filled our car, closed some years ago. I cannot imagine that it would have been pleasant (or even healthy) living in houses or flats so close to the fumes of petrol and other motor fuels.

The absence of shops in HGS was to a small extent compensated for by the visits of itinerant suppliers. Daily, electric milk floats left the Express Dairy depot on Hoop Lane and delivered milk (in glass bottles with foil tops) to our front porch. As they moved, one could hear their bottles rattling against each other. When I was at Golders Hill School (see above), pupils were encouraged to save the used foil bottle tops and to bring them into school, where they were bagged up and sent to the Doctor Barnardo's charity, which sold them to raise money. We were also given colourfully painted stiff cardboard boxes shaped like houses to collect money at home. When we brought the money into school, we were rewarded with metal brooches provided by the charity. The milk floats also carried cream, yoghurt, bread, and orange juice. Newspapers were also delivered to our front door every day by an employee, usually a teenaged school pupil, of WH Smiths in Temple Fortune.

A travelling shop brought vegetables to the HGS. This was in a shabby, old lorry driven by a grumpy man, who sold his produce from the back of his vehicle. My mother, who preferred buying vegetables elsewhere, made infrequent use of this service. A keen disciple of the pioneering promoter of Mediterranean cuisine, Elizabeth David (1913-1992), and herself a gourmet cook, she preferred buying our food from continental stores in Old Compton Street in Soho. Every now and then, Hampstead Way was visited by a Frenchman (wearing a beret) on a bicycle laden with strings of onions. My aunt in Raeburn Close was one of his faithful customers.

Occasionally, a knife sharpener arrived on his bicycle. I enjoyed watching the sparks flying off his pedal-powered grinding wheel as he sharpened knives, scissors, and garden shears. None of these belonged to us because my mother was dubious about his skills. Yet another regular to visit Hampstead Way and liven our almost silent lives was a horse-drawn scrap metal collector: a 'rag and bones' man. He and his mate used to make their presence felt by yelling something that sounded like: "Any old iron and echo." Incidentally, Peter Sellers (1925-1980) released a record of a song called "Any Old Iron" in 1957. Eventually, these men replaced their horse and cart with a motorised lorry, which looked little better than the discarded stuff they collected. With their 'new' vehicle, which they drove incredibly slowly, they continued to shout: 'Any old iron and echo."

Golders Green Library is about 0.7 miles from Central Square as the crow flies and much further by foot. Once or twice a week during my childhood, a mobile library, operated by the local borough council, arrived on South Square in the car park of St Jude's Church. It was a long caravan attached to truck of the kind used to pull articulated lorries. I visited it rarely, preferring the larger selection of books in the Golders Green library. It must have been a godsend for people who found it difficult to walk from the Suburb to the larger library.

Arcades below Arcade House in Temple Fortune

In the early 1960s, my parents installed central heating into number 36. It was powered by a boiler that burnt anthracite. An open-backed lorry delivered the fuel to us at regular intervals. The coal was packed in long cylindrical sacks, which the dust-covered coal deliverers carried on their backs to the pair of brick storage bunkers next to the rear wall of our garage. They had been specially built for my parents by a local builder.

Later in the 1960s, my parents had a Permutit water-softening system installed. I could never understand why, but my parents told me that with softened water, one used less soap. Softened water also reduces the rate that pipes fur up with calcium deposits. Once a week, the unit containing the ion-exchange resins had to be refreshed with dendritic salt. In the 1960s, sacks of this special form of $NaCl$ were only delivered by Harrods of Knightsbridge. The deliveries were made in silently running electrically powered vans. To have these deliveries, the family had to have an account with Harrods. This reminds me of something, which although it is a digression, I will now relate. Harrods has never been a store that one would enter hoping to find a bargain. In the sixties, they provided their customers with very attractive carrier bags. My late mother liked these, but she was not particularly interested in buying anything from the store in Knightsbridge. So, she used to enter Harrods and buy a packet of Polo mints, one of the least costly things on sale, and have the payment of them put on the family account. This low-cost purchase allowed her to get what she really wanted: a Harrods' carrier bag.

The HGS Trust tries (mostly successfully) to ensure that the external appearance of buildings within the Suburb are kept as they were originally designed. Each of the wood framed windows of our house, like many others in the Suburb, contained a latticework of small panes of glass. My late mother decided that the wooden dividers running between the panes dramatically reduced the amount of light entering our rooms. So, without consulting anyone in charge of the suburb's appearance, she had the latticed windows overlooking the garden replaced with new windows, each containing large single sheets of sealed double-layer insulating glass. This was done in the 1960s. Several years after this was done, our house appeared on the front page of the Suburb's annual report, which was circulated to every household. The picture had been taken because it included our apple tree in glorious full blossom. Our 'illegal' windows were clearly visible beyond the blossoms. Nothing happened until the 1980s, some years after my mother died. Then, my father received a letter from the Trust, noting that our house had the wrong kind of windows and that they should be restored to the original design. My father replied something like this:

"I am sorry to hear that we have infringed the regulations, but I used to leave matters such as the management of the house in the hands of my dear late wife."

And that was the end of that. He was never troubled again by the Trust. After he sold our house in about 1992, its new owners restored the offending windows to the satisfaction of the Trust by replacing the sheet glass with the small panes separated by wooden lattices. It was not only our house that infringed the conservation rules. One of our neighbours on Hampstead Way surreptitiously added a small brick side porch. They were ordered to demolish it immediately, which they did.

Our nearest Underground station was Golders Green. Until the end of my teens, there used to be an entrance to it from under the bridge across Finchley Road (opposite the Artista). This entrance was reached by walking along a passageway beneath an elaborately constructed canopy supported by wooden pillars. In the 1970s, a well-travelled visitor, who was visiting our house, told me that the woodwork reminded him of structures he had seen in India. This covered way led to a ticket hall. Neither the passageway, which still exits, nor the ticket hall have been accessible to the public for many years.

Harold Wilson (1916-1995), who was Prime Minister twice, lived in Southway (number 12) until 1964. I never met him, but once I met one of his ministers Patrick Gordon-Walker (1907-1980) at a party held by an US diplomat and his family, the Zacharias's, who lived on South Square in a house next to a path that leads to Hill Close. Their daughter 'Missy' was a good friend of my sister. Many other famous people were living in the Suburb when I lived there. I met a few of them, especially those who were my father's colleagues.

My father was an academic (an economist) at the London School of Economics ('LSE'). Several LSE academics lived in the HGS, some having moved there before my father moved in, and others later. The sociologist Percy Cohen lived close to us at the top of Hill Close. The economist and good friend of the family Sir Lionel Robbins (1898-1984) lived between us and the Heath Extension on Meadway Close. My father's PhD supervisor, the economist Sir Arnold Plant (1898-1978) lived in a house on the edge of the Extension near where Wildwood Road and Kingsley Way meet. The statistician Claus Moser (1922-2015) lived in Linnell Close when I was small: we visited his family for mid-morning coffee occasionally. Further south along Wildwood Road, there is a small cul-de-sac called Turners Wood. It was here that the eminent philosopher Imre Lakatos (1922-1974) lived until his untimely death. Our family socialised a great deal with Lakatos and his partner, as well as with the Robbins. The philosopher John Watkins (1924-1999) and his family lived in Erskine Hill. John was a keen chess player and a friend of the poet Dannie Abse (1923-2014), who lived in Golders Green, and wrote about the place. I met him briefly once or twice at the Watkins when Dannie was playing Chess with John. In his autobiography, Abse wrote:

"I played chess with my philosopher friend from LSE, John Watkins, and swallowed hard, wearing that blank loser's smile, whenever he gloated 'checkmate'"

John's son Hugh and I attended the same preparatory school in Swiss Cottage (The Hall School), and we have been friends ever since we met there in about 1960. When I walked to Golders Green station on my way to school, I often walked with Professor Ben Roberts (also taught at LSE), who lived in Temple Fortune Lane near the actor Donald Sinden (1923-2014), whom I never met but I spotted occasionally. Nobel Prize winning economist Friedrich Von Hayek (1899-1992), a refugee from Nazi Germany, also lived in the Suburb. His house was in Constable Close, near Lionel Robbins and Arnold Plant, but that was in the 1930s, long before I was born.

Many famous economists visited us at 36 Hampstead Way. So, as a youngster, without really appreciating it, I was then socialising with many academics who have made significant advances in economics and related subjects, and in one case a future Prime Minister of Italy: my father's MSc student Romano Prodi.

Despite interesting encounters made when my parents entertained a variety of fascinating friends (including those already mentioned as well as the sculptors Elizabeth Frink, Menashe Kadishman, and Buki Schwarz), life for me as a child in HGS was not particularly scintillating. My late mother used to take my sister and me into the West End regularly. Seeing the exciting, bustling, and vibrant activity in central London made me realise more and more how dull life in the HGS was in comparison. This might sound awful and even ungrateful, but that is how I felt. Today, people might even kill to be able to afford a home in the still highly desirable HGS, but not me. If money were no object and I was to move back to NW11, I would now prefer to live in Golders Green in one of the roads near to Golders Hill Park.

Sam Stoller kosher fish shop in Temple Fortune

AFTERWORD

The poet and physician Mark Akenside (1721-1770) was a friend of the politician Jeremiah Dyson (1722-1776), who had his house in Golders Green. A regular visitor to Dyson's home, Akenside wrote, while recovering from an ailment:

> "Thy verdant scenes, O Goulder's Hill,
>
> Once more I seek a languid guest;
>
> With throbbing temples and with burden'd breast
>
> Once more I climb thy steep aerial way,
>
> O faithful cure of oft-returning ill …"

These words were written long before Finchley Road traversed the fields at Golders Green. For the poet and his friend, Golders Green was merely a few houses strung along what is now Golders Green Road, as it headed towards the bridge across the River Brent, and beyond it Hendon. The road still exists, and water, some of it supplied by Mutton Brook, continues to flow under the bridge. Everything else would be unrecognisable to Dyson and his poetic guest. Finchley Road was built after both men had passed away, and many years after that, the Underground arrived close to where Golders Green and Finchley Road meet. The arrival of the railway in 1907 was to transform the hamlet of Golders Green into the thriving suburb that it has become.

The word 'arcadia' is included in the title of this book. It is commonly understood to mean a utopian or idealised vision of pastoral or rural life. Prior to the earliest years of the 20th century, Golders Green and its surroundings, such as the banks of Mutton Brook and the Brent, as well as the fields and woods where Hampstead Garden Suburb stands today, were close to being arcadian. When people began moving out to live in newly developing suburbs such as Golders Green, they were lured by the prospect of living in an environment near to real countryside, Developers claimed it to be a sort of arcadia. Golders Green and Hampstead Garden Suburb are no longer close to London's countryside. However, their proximity to arcadian open spaces like Hampstead Heath, Golders Hill Park, and Kenwood, justify residents' feelings that they are within easy reach of places where, at least for a short while, they can imagine that they have realised their quest for the pastoral idyll.

My book has described Golders Green, its neighbour the Hampstead Garden Suburb as they were in their early days before my birth, during my childhood, and in the present. I hope that my text has helped to make the area and its history more interesting to both its residents and to those who live beyond its boundaries. I have described places, some of which I have seen but no longer exist. Like most parts of London, Golders Green continues to change. The same cannot be said for its neighbour Hampstead Garden Suburb, whose appearance is protected by law and vigilant members of its managing trust.

While researching this book, I have looked at many websites, some of which might have been deleted or not kept up to date since I came across them, and several books, all mentioned in the text. Where possible, I have not relied on a single source of information but tried to cross-reference it. If you should chance upon any factual errors or inaccuracies in this volume, please regard them as accidental, and accept my apologies.

I have enjoyed writing this book for several reasons. One is that Golders Green is a relatively underrated place, about which there is little recently written in the form of topographical and travel literature. Another reason is that it has helped me recover memories of my childhood, and, I hope, those of others in my age group who have experienced living in Golders Green and the Suburb. Thirdly, a chance comment made by a friend who lives near Golders Green made me realise that many of the area's inhabitants, who have taken its history and features for granted, might like to know more about it. It was her few words that made me 'set pen to paper' to enlighten you about a small area of northwest London, which a London Transport poster of 1908 described as "A place of delightful prospects."

Golders Hill Park
Top: bandstand. Bottom: deer resting

SOME BOOKS CONSULTED

Abse, D: "Goodbye, twentieth century: an autobiography" (publ. 2001)

Cherry, B & Pevsner, N: "The Buildings of England. London 4: North" (publ. 1998)

Clayton, E: "Barbara Hepworth. Art and Life" (publ. 2021)

Duveen, JH: "The Rise of the House of Duveen" (publ. 1957)

Fox, P: "The Jewish Community of Golders Green" (publ. 2016)

Gilbert, M: "The Boys" (publ. 1996)

Griffiths, J: "Henrietta Barnett and Her First Class High School" (publ. 2013)

Hastings, S: "Evelyn Waugh" (publ. 1994)

How, J & M: "St. Edward the Confessor Parish, Golders Green London N.W.11: 100 Years of Parish History" (publ. 2009-12)

Howkins, F: "The Story of Golders Green" (publ. 1923)

Julius, A: "Trials of the Diaspora. A history of Anti-Semitism in England" (publ. 2010)

Miller, M: "Hampstead Garden Suburb" (publ. 1995)

Pfefferkorn, E: "The Muselmann at the Water Cooler…" (publ. 2012)

Reid, A: "Brentham: A history of the pioneer garden suburb 1901-2001" (publ. 2000)

Ridley, J: "The Architect and his Wife" (publ. 2002)

Smith, CR & Hall JP: "The Story of Golders Green" (publ. 1979)

Thorne, J: "Handbook to The Environs of London" (publ. 1876)

Unwin, R: "Town Planning in Practice" (publ. 1909)

Walford, E: "Old and New London: Volume 5" (publ. 1878)

Watkins, M: "Henrietta Barnett in Whitechapel" (publ. 2005)

Waugh, E: "A Little Learning" (publ. 1964)

Yamey, A: "Beneath a Wide Sky: Hampstead and its Environs" (publ. 2022)

Note: If inadvertently I have infringed any copyright issues, please accept my sincerest apologies.

All photographs were taken by the author.

ACKNOWLEDGEMENTS

Thanks are due to the following, none of whom can be held in the least bit responsible for any errors or omissions in my text:

Bridie (wherever she is), the late Harold Hodes, Micky Watkins, my cousins David and Jane Rindl, David Klappholz, Martin and Kiran Pidd, and Christine Rafferty.

My dear wife Lopa deserves much gratitude for her patience and help while I was writing this book and for accompanying me on many expeditions from Kensington to Golders Green and Hampstead Garden Suburb.

Roof tops on Golders Green Road

A sun dial in Hampstead Gerden Suburb
(North Square)

South side of Golders Green Road looking towards the war memorial clock tower

INDEX

A

ABC cinema 70, 83
Abse, Danny 192
Aida Foster Stage School 119
Alba Lodge 79
Albert Row 42, 78
Alyth Gardens 58
Alyth synagogue 119
Annandale House 133, 135
anti-aircraft guns 166
anti-apartheid 72
Antisemitism 62, 177
Appenrodt's 58
Arcade House 120, 126, 185, 188
Art Deco 16, 24, 124–125, 161, 163–164
Artisans Quarter 147
Artista 71, 73, 115, 191
Arts and Craft Movement 161
Arup, Ove 172
Aumonier, Eric 16

B

Baeck, Leo 104
Bamboo Bar 70, 73, 115
Bar Linda 112
Barnett, Henrietta 142, 175, 180
Basing, Adam de 14
Beecholme's Bakery 58, 91
Belvedere Court 19, 106, 163
Big Wood 158, 179
Bigwood Road 86
Birnbeck Court 125
Bishops Avenue 19

Blooms 69
Bolshevik 85
bombs 166
Boots 123
bowling alley 110
Braikevitch, MV 83
Brent Bridge 37, 77
Brent Bridge Hotel 37
Brent Bridge House 36–37
Brent River Park 31
Brentford 8, 13
Brentford Nylons 122
Brentham garden suburb 145
Brick Lane 78
Bridge Lane 30
Broadwalk Lane 68
Brooklands Drive 25

C

cannabis 123
Carmelite Monastery 31
Carmelli's 68
Census 2011 62
Central Hotel 99
Central Square 149, 175
Chabad house 86
Charing Cross 43
Cherry Tree Wood 14
Chiang Kai-shek 131
Childs Hill 46, 109
Chinese restaurants 91, 124, 131
church bells 185
Clock tower 97
Clough, John (Dr) 115
Coates, Eric 172
Cock in Hoop Ale House 92
Cohens (delicatessen) 24
College Farm 14
Constable Close 193
Country Market 68
covid19 131, 161

Cowper, William 8
Crittall 24, 163–164

D

Daniels' Bagel Bakery 122
Decoy Pond 32–33
Dollis Brook 8, 30
Ducksetters Lane 31
Dunstan Road 52, 132
Duveen 49

E

Eagle Lodge 55, 81–83
East Finchley Station 16
Edward the Confessor 99, 119
elephants 159
Ernest Owers 50, 105
Express Dairy 100, 186
extension of Northern Line 43–44, 51

F

Falloden Way 25
Fellowship House 173
finger post 95, 98
Fox, Pam 49
Franks 66
Free Church 151–152, 173
Free Church Hall 158
Freshwater Hostel 60
Freud, Ernst 19, 106
Freud, Sigmund 19, 101
Friends Meeting House 154, 157
Frink, Elizabeth 193
Frohwein's 122

G

Garden Suburb Junior School 173–174
Garrick, David 40
Glentree 99
Golders Green Club 119
Golders Green Crematorium 100
Golders Green Library 86, 187
Golders Green Police Station 31
Golders Green public library 88
Golders Green Station bus yard 127
Golders Green Synagogue 51–52
Golders Green telephone exchange 99
Golders Green war memorial 6
Golders Hill Park 137, 144, 179, 185, 198
Golders Hill School 116, 118, 186
Golders Hill Terrace 134–135
Goldfinger, Erno 96–97, 132
Gordon-Walker, Patrick 191
Gothic Cottages 74, 77
Great Wall 148–149, 175, 180
Greek Orthodox Cathedral of the Holy Cross & St. Michael 87, 89–90
Grodzinski's 56, 79
Gryn, Hugo 104
Guedalla, Philip 104

H

H2 bus 180
Hampstead 43
Hampstead Garden Suburb 141

Hampstead Garden Suburb Trust 145
Hampstead Golf Club 176
Hampstead Heath Extension 147–148
Hampstead Heath Protection Fund 144
Hampstead Way 171, 173, 179, 182
Hampstead Way, 36 183
Hannukah 62
Harrods 189
Hawthorns, The 49
Hayek, Friedrich von 193
Heath End House 143
Heath Extension Council 144
Heathgate 151, 175
Hendrix, Jimi 112
Henlys Corner 26
Henrietta Barnett memorial 155–156
Henrietta Barnett School 155
Hepworth, Barbara 136
Hess, Myrah 176
Highfield Road 77
Hill Close 172, 183
Hillsong Church 130
Hippodrome theatre 127–128
Hitchens, Ivor 100
Hodford Farm 42
Hodford Road 92
Hoop Lane 46, 51, 92, 99, 171
Howard, Ebenezer 142
Howkins, Francis 39

I

Importers 67
Institute, The 153, 155
Ionic cinema 70, 111
Ivy House 137, 140

J

Jaegers 71
Japanese 125
Jewish 49
Jewish Cemetery 51, 103, 171
Jewish refugees 59
Jewish Vegetarian Society 60, 111
Joseph's bookstore 122

K

Kanu 122
Kendricks 122
King Alfred School 136
Kingsley Close 24, 163
Kingsley Way bridge 12, 21
Kinloss Schul (synagogue) 27, 29
Klappholz, Kurt 60
knife sharpener 187
Kosher Kingdom 79
Kosher meat 57
Krasin, Leonid 102

L

La Délivrance 28–29
Lakatos, Imre 176, 192
Landy's 123
Little Wood 158–159
Little Wood theatre 160
Litvinov, Maxim 85
Lloyd-George, David 29, 44
London School of Economics ('LSE') 191
Lutyens, Edwin 102, 149, 157, 167, 184
Lyttelton Playing Fields 21–22

Lytton Close 162, 164

M

M&S Foodhall 124
Mac Fishery 68
Mac Market 68
Machzide Hadath synagogue 76, 78
Madame Leiberg 59
Mademoiselle Nicolaeva 86
Manor House Hospital 137
Markaz El Tathgheef El Eslami 130
Market Place 24, 165, 185
Maurice and Vivien Wohl Campus 80, 82
McDonalds 16
Meadway 119, 171
Meadway Court 168, 175
Medtner, N 84
Menachem's 79
Mendel's garage 185
Met Su Yan 91
Metz, Maurice de 20
Meyer, Bruno 85
Middleton Road 117
milestone 110
Milligan, Spike 103
Moser, Claus 192
Mutton Brook 13, 21, 25, 34, 159

N

Name 'Golders Green' 40
National Express 50
New Delhi 150
Norrice Lea 20, 58
North Circular Road 29, 35, 77
North Square 157, 203

Northern Line 43

O

Odeon cinema 124
Old Bull and Bush pub 179
Old White Lion pub 16
onions 187
Orchard, The 169, 172

P

Pantiles, The 125
pantomime 127
Panzers 123
Parker, Richard 145
Parkway Patisserie 132
Pavlova 137
Pavlova, Anna 84, 101, 111
Peking Duck 124
Permutit 189
Pevsner, Nikolaus 51
Pfefferkorn, Eli 61
Phoenix Cinema 16
Pick, Frank 175, 178
Platters Deli 122
Play and Pageant Union 159
Pogroms 85
Pollitt, Harry 102
Potter, Harry 151
Prince Albert pub 78
Princess Margaret 155
Prodi, Romano 193
Pullens 120

R

Rachmaninov 84
Raeburn Close 178, 184
rag and bones 187
Refectory, The 112, 114
Regal cinema 110
Repton, Humphrey 138

Rindl, Sven 136
River Brent 30
Robbins, Lionel 175, 192
Robeson, Paul 102
Rodborough Road 92
Rotherwick Road 171, 180
Royal Oak pub 123
Russian People's Embassy 86
Russians 83

S

Sainsbury's 68, 111
Sainsburys 70
Sam Stoller 122–123, 194
Schreuer 100, 184
Shiras Devorah school 119
Shree Swaminarayan Temple 110
Shutlers 121
Sinden, Donald 192
skating rink 110
Solly's 69
Solomon, Digby 52
South Square 157
Spaghetti House 71, 115
Springer, Jerry 20
St Albans church 132
St Albans Church Hall 52, 65–66, 129
St Anthony's School for Girls 137
St Jude's Church 151, 154, 185
St Michael's 87
St Ninian 110
Steigman 58
Sunshine Corner 175
supermarket 68

T

Taylor, Elizabeth 175
Tea House 173
Temple Fortune 30, 46, 120, 188, 194
Temple Fortune Farm 30
Temple Fortune House 120, 126
Temple Fortune Lane 181, 184
Tesco's 68
The Castle pub 109
Tomchinski, Minna 86
trams 67
Trinity Church 92–93
trolleybuses 67
Tung Hsing 131
Turners Wood 176
Tutu, Desmond 132

U

Ultra-orthodox Judaism 62, 64
Underhill 135
Unitarian Church 100
United Synagogue (Hamp. Gdn. Sub.) 20
Unwin, Raymond 145, 165, 179
Upmarket shops 71

V

Vadgama, Kusum 120
Vivian House 120
Vivian, Henry 146

W

Wade, Charles 149
Waitrose 123

war memorial 97

Waugh, Evelyn 9, 39, 98, 135
Wellgarth Nursery Training College 136, 139
Wellgarth Road 135–136
WH Smiths 121, 186
Whishaw 37
White Swan pub 75, 78
Whitechapel Art Gallery 143
WHSmith 123
Wild Hatch 165, 181
Wildwood Road 175, 182
Willifield Green 173
Willifield Way 172
Wilson, Harold 175–176, 191
Wolff, Samuel 51
Woolworths 69–70
Wyldes Farm 179

Y

Yerkes, Charles Tyson 44–45

Printed in Great Britain
by Amazon